Bus Stations in Britain

THE FIFTIES TO THE EIGHTIES

Front cover: Folkestone bus station in Bouverie Square opened in July 1955 on a site which previously consisted of tennis courts surrounded by trees. After refurbishment in 2004 the bus station remains in situ although in recent years there have been proposals to redevelop the site since it is on the edge of a major shopping centre (Bouverie Place). However, these plans have not materialised largely due to the difficulty in finding an alternative location for the bus station. The former East Kent Road Car Company office building in the centre background still stands (but without the lettering), as does the former Central Post Office building (background left) dating from 1937. The bus in the foreground is a 1962 Park Royal-bodied AEC Regent V, registration YJG 814, and this picture was taken around 1963. (Phil Tatt/Online Transport Archive)

Back cover: In this view at Stockport dating from August 1981 Greater Manchester Transport (GMT) buses monopolise the bus station apart from Trent 210, a Leyland National working Buxton service 199. In the background beyond the railway viaduct GMT's Daw Bank garage and workshops are visible. In the foreground is GMT Metrobus 5018 while behind the Trent vehicle is a former North Western Alexander-bodied RELL 324. The remaining three buses in full view are Park Royal-bodied Standards but the one on the extreme right is Northern Counties-bodied. (Geoff Morant)

Title page: This is a late 1950s view of Bournemouth bus station bursting with Hants & Dorset buses. About to depart is a 1948-built ECW- bodied Bristol L6A which is filled to the gunnels. Numbered 772 (previously TS 841), the bus was withdrawn by Hants & Dorset in 1964. In the background is the art deco Plummer Roddis department store in Old Christchurch Road dating from 1938. Rebranded Debenhams in 1972 and closed in the following year Roddis House is now occupied by several retailers. (Phil Tatt/Online Transport Archive)

First published 2021

ISBN 978 1 85414 456 0

Published by
Capital Transport Publishing Ltd
www.capitaltransport.com

Printed by Parksons Graphics

KEVIN McCORMACK

Bus Stations in Britain

THE FIFTIES TO THE EIGHTIES

Capital Transport

INTRODUCTION

This album depicts views of selected bus stations, both large and small, in England, Scotland and Wales photographed in colour from the late 1950s up to de-regulation in 1986. Most of the photographs will never have been seen before. In addition, the book seeks to provide a geographical spread so that a variety of bus types and liveries can be seen. The images in the main body of the book have been organised by letter of the alphabet. In most cases bus stations are pictured just once but in a few cases there are two or three images featuring different parts of the same bus station or replacement facilities. An index of locations is provided on the last page.

What actually constitutes a "bus station" is not always obvious except in cases where the signage describes the location in those words. However, for the purposes of this book "street loading" has been disregarded, the emphasis being on off street areas containing some infrastructure (shelters, waiting rooms etc) and preferably with potential passengers in evidence.

Many of today's bus station sites were established in the 1930s because some Councils were becoming concerned about excessive congestion caused by street stands serving increasing numbers of bus services. Most of these early bus stations were very basic, with some lasting into the 1950s and 60s, as evidenced in this album, and some replacement ones from later periods are also deemed unsuitable today. Many of these bus stations have since been abandoned, rebuilt or replaced by facilities in a different part of the town or city. There are a number of reasons for these changes including:

- value of land which can be put to so-called better use
- bus operators preferring street stops to save costs
- reduction in bus usage
- legislation requiring improved access for the elderly and disabled
- health and safety requirements for passengers, eg wider walkways and safer bus reversing areas
- desirability of having a more modern and inviting gateway to a particular town or city, often providing an interchange with other modes of transport.

However, many of the new bus stations, as well as the earlier generation ones still existing, do little to encourage bus travel although there are some exceptions, such as Barnsley, Blackburn, Norwich and Warrington. These are too modern to feature in this book which concentrates on a period when passengers' expectations were less sophisticated.

Most of the photographs in this book have been provided by the Online Transport Archive, a registered charity of which I am a trustee which was founded to preserve and conserve transport–related colour slides, cine films, negatives and prints. Special thanks go to my fellow trustees, Charles Roberts and Peter Waller, for their help in finding and enhancing appropriate photographic material and to various individual contributors including Chris Evans, Alan Murray, Mike Russell, John Bath, Mike Greenwood, Jonathan Cadwallader, Roger Barton, Garry Ward, Margaret Seaton, Don Akrigg, Gavin Booth, Russ Jarvis, Malcolm Keeley, Thomas Knowles and Mike Eyre for providing photographs and/or information. I should also thank James Whiting of Capital Transport for sourcing some pictures.

Finally, I would like to acknowledge a particularly useful website, Bus Lists on the Web, for information relating to particular vehicles and Google Street View for current location checking.

Kevin R McCormack
Ashtead, Surrey, March 2021

The windows are steaming up as passengers sit inside Red & White L362 waiting to leave Abergavenny bus station in Monmouthshire. Red & White Services opened this bus station in Monmouth Road in 1931 and the original building is still standing, but now used for other purposes. The bus station remains in place but has been reconfigured and reduced in size, with just five bays and two shelters. However, there is a cafe on site and toilets are available in the adjacent car park. The corner of the toilet block is in fact visible on the left of this picture. L362 is an ECW-bodied Bristol Lodekka FS6G built in 1962, renumbered L6962 in 1975 and withdrawn in 1977. The Western Welsh vehicle is No 1323, a 1964 Willowbrook-bodied Leyland Tiger Cub. At the back is a Red & White MW, No U362, from 1963. Red & White Services, which was founded in 1929, became part of the National Bus Company (NBC) in 1969 and was merged with Western Welsh in 1978. (RWA Jones/Online Transport Archive)

Against the backdrop of Accrington's Grade II listed Market House opened in 1869, Accrington Corporation 155 and Rossendale Transport Leyland Leopard No 60 take on passengers in this early 1970s photograph. No 155 is a Leyland PD2/31 built in 1960 which was transferred to newly formed Hyndburn Borough Council in 1974 following a local government reorganisation. The Accrington bus station seen here was located in Peel Street alongside the outdoor market in front of the Market House (and largely concealing its facade). A new bus station opened in 2016 in King Street/ Edgar Street. (David Christie)

This is the Graham Street bus station in Airdrie, North Lanarkshire, in September 1970, just before it was relocated to Gartlea Road. However, this has since closed and Airdrie now has no bus station. The one seen here is now the location of the Sheriff Court but the buildings behind the bus in Graham Street, close to Baillies roundabout, are still extant. The bus is a Leyland PD2/41 with a lowbridge Massey body delivered in 1959. It is carrying the livery of Baxter's Motor Services (originally their No 70) but is actually Eastern Scottish HH38 in this photograph. Baxter's of Airdrie started operations in 1914 and remained independent until acquisition by Eastern Scottish on 1 December 1962. The painting of Baxter's fleet into the new owner's green livery caused an outcry and so the vehicles reverted to blue and grey livery with the Baxter fleetname until the late 1970s. (Alan Murray-Rust/ Online Transport Archive)

Seen here in the early 1960s Aldershot bus station in Station Road had nine loading bays and opened in 1933. It has since been moved to the right of this picture, adjacent to the railway station, and the original site redeveloped for mainly residential use. However, there are now plans to build on the current bus station. This picture features two Aldershot & District (A&D) buses. On the left is No 875, a Guy Arab II originally built in 1943 and rebodied by Weymann in 1950. The bus is parked next to No 203, an East Lancs-bodied Dennis Lance K4, new in 1954. Aldershot & District Traction was merged with Thames Valley Traction on 1 January 1972 to form Alder Valley. (John May/ Online Transport Archive)

Ashton-under-Lyne bus station has been subject to four incarnations and this picture depicts the first version built in 1963 with six loading bays and the usual narrow platforms. To keep pace with nearby retail developments the bus station was modernised in 1983-5 and again in 1994. Finally, with the arrival of Metrolink a combined bus and tram interchange has been created adjacent to the old site and this opened in 2020. In this view from c.1970 four different bus liveries are on show, yet all the vehicles belong to South East Lancashire North East Cheshire Passenger Transport Executive (SELNEC). Nearest the camera is No 3137, a Leyland Atlantean delivered to Salford Corporation in 1968 which was their No 291. Salford was one of eleven municipalities whose bus fleet was transferred into newly-created SELNEC on 1 November 1969 and is still wearing Salford livery. On the right is SELNEC 6230, a 1965 Weymann-bodied Daimler Fleetline, formerly Rochdale No 330 and still in the Corporation's livery. Next in line is former Stockport Corporation 9, a Leyland PD2A carrying its new SELNEC livery and numbered 5809. Furthest away is a Daimler Fleetline still in Manchester livery. (Howard J Piltz/Online Transport Archive)

In May 2007, Barnsley Interchange opened, a dramatic looking, award winning combined rail and bus facility. Yet, there has been a bus station here in Eldon Street for decades on the same site close to the railway station. An earlier station known until 1960 as Barnsley Exchange closed in 1973 and was replaced by a smaller one fifty yards away which was renamed Barnsley Interchange in 2007. The bus station has of course been reconfigured over the years and the 1977 version depicted here in October 1985 replaced the standard exposed version with buses lined up behind each other rather than parked in herringbone formation. There is a proliferation of National Bus Company (NBC) Poppy red livery in this view of Yorkshire Traction buses so the red and white variant carried by the Leyland Olympian in the foreground is a welcome break from the monotony. (Mike Greenwood)

This row of Bristol Omnibus Company Bristol single and double deckers is standing in Bath bus station in Manvers Street. This bus station opened in 1958 and the original layout had buses standing in line occupying platforms but, as seen here, was subsequently remodelled to enable buses to reverse onto the stands. It was demolished in July 2007 and replaced by a new bus station in Dorchester Street which opened in June 2009 adjacent to the Southgate shopping centre. In the intervening two years a temporary bus station was created on a car park in Avon Street. The bus nearest the camera is No 7023, a Bristol FLF 6B Lodekka with ECW bodywork built in 1961. The spire protruding above the buildings belongs to St John the Evangelist church in South Parade and dates from 1867. (Geoff Pullin/Online Transport Archive)

In the shadow of the All Hallows multi-storey car park in Bedford during 1963 an almost new United Counties Bristol Lodekka, No 634, waits for passengers at the bus station. This was created following an exchange of land in 1957 with United Counties surrendering its small bus station in the Broadway and receiving from the Council the plot of land seen here. The bus station was later modernised, with the enclosing of the open passenger waiting area with glass screens and the buses were then parked facing the building. Eventually the station came to be regarded as an outdated gateway to the town and was closed for redevelopment in 2014. The new bus station opened on 29 March 2015. United Counties became part of NBC in 1969 and was acquired by Stagecoach in 1987. Indeed, the United Counties name on the building above the roof of the bus came to be replaced by Stagecoach branding. (Geoff Pullin/Online Transport Archive)

Above: When this picture was taken in the mid-1960s Birkenhead Woodside bus station was a major transport hub serving the ferry terminal to Liverpool and, out of view on the right, the massive railway terminus with twin train shed roofs providing through trains to London Paddington. The railway station closed in November 1967, a victim of the Beeching Axe, and the main bus station moved to Conway Street in the centre of Birkenhead in 1996. A small bus station exists roughly where the photographer is standing and between that and the ferry terminal (now a listed building dating from 1864) is a tram terminus. This is the half-mile long system serving the Wirral Transport Museum in Taylor Street. The bus nearest the camera is Birkenhead Corporation Daimler Fleetline No 107 which was new in September 1964. The Corporation bus fleets of Birkenhead, Wallasey and Liverpool were amalgamated to form Merseyside Passenger Transport Executive on 1 December 1969. The tall dark building on the skyline is Liverpool's Grade I Listed Liver Building at Pier Head. (Roy Marshall/The Bus Archive)

Above right: Boulevard bus station in Blackburn had stands in front of and opposite the railway station and these two pictures depict the section opposite the station. The area around the Grade II Listed railway station has since been transformed into the Cathedral Square complex and a six-storey office block and piazza now occupy the old bus station site. This 1970 view features Blackburn Corporation 134, a 1949 Crossley-bodied Guy Arab III in plain Corporation livery without the original intricate lining. An identical bus, No 133, has been preserved. (David Christie)

Right: In this view of the other section of Blackburn bus station looking towards Railway Road, the buildings in the background have been demolished except the light coloured one behind the No Entry sign. Boulevard bus station closed in September 2013 and a delayed new one opened in May 2016 in the area of Ainsworth Street and Salford (a road name). While it looks very modern and impressive, the old one at least created a railway/bus interchange unlike the new facility. In 1974, the municipal fleets of Blackburn and Darwen merged and the bus livery changed. However, the buses seen here are in Blackburn Corporation livery as the photograph was probably taken in 1970/1. They are, from left to right: No 118, a 1948 all-Leyland PD1A, Nos 64 and 18, Leyland Tiger Cubs, and No 53, a 1968 East Lancs-bodied Leyland Atlantean. (W Ryan/Online Transport Archive)

Passengers file on to West Monmouthshire Omnibus Board's Leyland Tiger Cub No 1, a 1964 PSUC1 with a Willowbrook body, at Blackwood's unattractive concrete bus station. West Mon was established in 1926 and its buses carried dark maroon livery until 1968 when the blue and white livery depicted here was introduced. As a result of local government reorganisation, West Mon became Islwyn Borough Transport in 1974 and at deregulation in 1986 became an arm's length company owned by Caerphilly County Borough Council. In January 2010 Caerphilly sold Islwyn to Stagecoach, the sale including its fleet of 33 buses and coaches. The bus station is located off Gordon Road behind the High Street in the indoor and outdoor market area and was rebuilt in the same location in 2007. (Roy Marshall/The Bus Archive)

Blackwood is situated in the Sirhowy Valley and is said to be the largest town in Wales not served by a railway. The updated Blackwood bus station is marketed as Blackwood Interchange but it is hard to imagine any direct interchange taking place with other means of public transport in the foreseeable future. However, there are rail-link bus services to other railway stations, the nearest being Ystrad Mynach, some twenty minutes away. Blackwood station was closed to passengers in 1960 making this "pre-Beeching" and the line was removed following closure to goods traffic in 1965. In this August 1977 view, three Leyland Leopards operated by Islwyn Borough Transport await departure at Blackwood. (RWA Jones/Online Transport Archive)

Here is one of Southdown's famous Leyland Titan PD3/5s, better known as Queen Marys due to their huge size compared with other buses of their era. This vehicle, dating from 1962 and bodied by Northern Counties, is No 915 running in disguise during the time when it temporarily surrendered its green and cream livery in favour of all-over advertising. It is promoting Roberts & Son's chain of off licences based in the south east, a business which had originated in Worthing in 1808. No 915 is pictured in January 1972 leaving Bognor Regis bus station in the High Street, a Southdown building with art deco facade which was erected in 1934 and demolished in 1993. Today, there is no trace of the bus station which was located at the upper end of the High Street although the site has not been built upon. In the midst of a few trees, a canopy bearing the name of Morrisons stands in its place leading to a large car park, at the far end of which is the supermarket. (Alan Murray-Rust/Online Transport Archive)

This is Howell Croft South in Bolton which opened as a combined bus and trolleybus station in July 1948. South Lancashire Transport (SLT) terminated its Leigh trolleybus service here and Lancashire United, Bolton and Bury Corporation buses also used the station. It closed in March 1969 with services relocated to Moor Lane bus station. The site of Howell Croft bus station is now occupied by the Octagon multi-storey car park. In this picture, SLT trolleybus 59, a Roe-bodied Leyland TTB4 originating in 1938, passes Bolton Transport 81, a Leyland PD2/13 built in 1956. The bus on the left is a Bolton Transport Crossley, distinguishable by the curved upper body band. Trolleybus 59 was withdrawn on 31 August 1958 which was the last day of trolleybus services in Bolton. The building with the conical roof in the background is the Gothic style offices of the Bolton Gas Company in Hotel Street which was demolished in 1963. (Phil Tatt/Online Transport Archive)

Moving across to Moor Lane bus station in Bolton we see two Lancashire United Guy Arab Vs, Nos 290 and 168 dating from 1967 and 1964 respectively, in the company of Greater Manchester PTE buses, just before the latter organisation took over Lancaster United in January 1976. This bus station opened in 1930, with the site doubling as a car park and fairground. Local services by Bolton Corporation, Ribble and Lancashire United plus the latter's tours and express services used the station. Closure came in September 2017 when it was replaced by Bolton Interchange in Newport Street. Over the years the bus station was periodically expanded and modernised. For example, the large steel bus shelters erected in 1969 were torn down in 1985. The clocktower dominating the background belongs to Bolton Town Hall in Victoria Square, a Grade II* listed building completed in 1873. (W Ryan/Online Transport Archive)

This is a bus station which suffered a premature demise due to a tyre store catching fire, the disaster being described in the local paper as a "£1m inferno". Luckily, nobody lost their life. Bournemouth's "Omnibus & Coach Station" on Exeter Road was built in Art Deco style in 1929-31 and was on two levels, with an underground coach station and a bus station at ground level. In 1959 the station was subject to a major rebuilding scheme to enable it to handle over 2000 vehicles and some 100,000 passengers per day. On 25 July 1976 a blaze destroyed the basement, along with sixteen coaches, but the surface bus station remained in use until 29 November 1980. In this view from September 1960 a Wilts & Dorset Bristol Lodekka, No 623, is just arriving. Standing on the right are two Hants & Dorset Bristol KSW6Bs, No 1305 and, in front, No 1308. (C Carter/Online Transport Archive)

In this second picture of Bournemouth bus station which was taken in August 1974 all the buses and coaches are carrying the Hants & Dorset fleet name following the merger with Wilts & Dorset in October 1972. The livery has changed to NBC Poppy red but some vehicles are still in the old green colours. The Wilts & Dorset name has been dropped but ironically H&D has adopted red which was W&D's colour rather than NBC Leaf green. Interestingly, the NBC fleetname is cream on the green buses to match the cream part of the old livery whereas on the red and white - liveried vehicles the fleetname is in white to match that livery. With the demise of the old bus station local buses now use a large number of street stands on both sides of Gervis Place/Old Christchurch Road, some of which are located in the shadow of the former Plummer building seen in the picture on the Title Page. A separate coach station has been created beside Bournemouth railway station and nearby Boscombe and Poole have bus stations. (Mike Greenwood)

Following the fire at Bournemouth's bus station on 25 July 1976 a temporary base was set up on the following day at the nearby Triangle, seen here crammed with buses and creating a logistical nightmare. A Hants & Dorset Motor Services member of staff appears to have arrived in ex-King Alfred 1970 Ford Transit minibus 2047 and has commandeered a local noticeboard in order to affix a timetable. King Alfred Motor Services ceased trading on 28 April 1973 and its fleet was acquired by Hants & Dorset. The only other identifiable bus is Bristol RELL6G No 3050 (originally 1646) built in 1971. Hants & Dorset and neighbouring Wilts & Dorset were taken over by the newly formed NBC on 1 January 1969 and were merged in 1972 under the Hants & Dorset name. (Geoff Morant)

This is Bradford's Chester Street bus station which was developed from the mid-1920s and closed when a new one was constructed alongside the repositioned Bradford Exchange railway station in 1977 (see next picture). This scene is virtually unrecognisable today due to road widening and the creation of a massive building incorporating Bradford Ice Arena resulting in the demolition of the buildings in the background in Little Horton Lane including the Chester Cafe, much frequented by bus crews. Indeed the only building which survives today is the one on the extreme right bearing the Bus Station signage which is currently a restaurant. The majority of people in the picture appear to have alighted from the Ledgard 1957 Daimler CVG6 with Burlingham bodywork. Samuel Ledgard started operating bus services in 1924 and following his death in 1952 his Executors operated the business until selling out to West Yorkshire in 1967, some of whose fleet can be seen behind the Daimler. (Phil Tatt/Online Transport Archive)

The new bus station called Bradford Interchange (also the name of the railway station since 1983) was built alongside the railway station and opened on 14 January 1977. Originally, the bus station had a "ridge and furrow" glass roof but this was removed in 1999 to allow for rebuilding with a reduction in size, which was completed in 2001. This picture was taken in April 1986 and shows West Yorkshire Passenger Transport Executive 5077, a 1983 Leyland Olympian with Roe bodywork, standing under the overall roof along with many more buses. Most of them, including No 5077, are in PTE "Metrobus" livery, a requirement following the creation of a joint venture company by the PTE and NBC called the Metro National Company. This arrangement ceased when deregulation occurred in Yorkshire in October 1986. (Mike Greenwood)

Brent Cross shopping centre in the London Borough of Barnet was the first stand-alone shopping centre in the UK and the forerunner of many such large out of town retail sites. It has stood the test of time well and it is perhaps hard to imagine that the centre and its associated bus station opened as early as March 1976. It has barely altered in outward appearance since then but the types of buses that serve it have of course changed. The seven LT buses on show here consist of pairs of RMLs and DMSs and three SMs. The taxi rank stands alongside Prince Charles Drive. Geographically, this general area has been known as Brent Cross for some time (the River Brent, which enters the River Thames at Brentford is close by) and the Cross is a reference to the cross roads where the North Circular Road (A406) bisected Hendon Way (A41) before the Brent Cross flyover was constructed. (Kevin Lane)

East Yorkshire Motor Services Park Royal-bodied AEC Renown No 781 has succumbed to NBC Poppy red in this view at Bridlington bus station. The vehicle has lost its previous blue and white livery which is recalled in the bus station's matching tiling and the gable end poster/route map. The bus dates from April 1965 and was sold by East Yorkshire for further use in November 1978, lasting into the current millennium before being dismantled to provide parts for the restoration of No 782. Bridlington bus station was built by East Yorkshire in the 1930s and closed in August 1984. The site is now occupied by The Promenades shopping centre in The Promenade (B1254) but the building behind, on the corner of Princess Terrace, is still extant. However, the gable end with the poster/map is now concealed by the shopping centre apart from the very top. If East Yorkshire's advertisement still existed, it would now be on the side of Boots Pharmacy. (W Ryan/Online Transport Archive)

There is an array of bus liveries on display in this scene at Old Steine, Brighton, from the mid-1970s, partly caused by various reorganisations of the bus companies serving Brighton around this time. Until the arrival of NBC in 1969, Brighton Corporation buses and those of Brighton, Hove and District (BH&D) wore the same red and cream livery, the only difference being that the former carried the Borough crest. On 1 January 1969 BH&D was absorbed into Southdown which started to paint the ex- BH&D vehicles into its green livery. Also, from June 1970 the Corporation changed its bus livery to blue and white. In this view, the vehicle beside the Platform 1 sign is Corporation Leyland Atlantean 87 from 1972 in all over advertising livery, in the centre is Corporation 29, a Leyland PD2/37 built in 1965, and on the right is ex-BH&D Bristol Lodekka 63, also from 1965, which displays its Southdown livery and fleet number 2063. The red and cream buses behind would soon lose their traditional Brighton colours. This location at Old Steine had been used as a terminal point for trams until 1939 and trolleybuses until 1959-61. Buses still terminate here but there is no infrastructure remaining. The backdrop remains unchanged today.

Buses in Burnley used to congregate on the site of the old cattle market until the concrete bus station seen here was built in 1964. This lasted until replaced on the same site by a new one of futuristic design which opened in October 2002. This picture depicts Leyland National No 136 dating from 1974 sporting a special livery to recognise HM The Queen's Silver Jubilee, 1952-1977. The other vehicle, a Bristol RES6L built in 1971, is wearing traditional red and cream colours. In 1933, the Burnley, Colne and Nelson Joint Transport Committee was formed to bring together the transport operations of these three municipalities. In 1974, the boroughs of Colne and Nelson were merged to form Pendle, resulting in a name change to Burnley and Pendle for the Joint Committee. The assets were transferred to a new arm's length company in 1986 and Pendle sold its share to Stagecoach in 1996, with Burnley following in 1997. (W Ryan/Online Transport Archive)

While some towns are keen to promote their street bus termini as bus stations (Colchester being a current example) Burton-on-Trent went in the opposite direction and referred to their bus station as a bus park. This is Wetmore Bus Park in October 1977 featuring a Leyland Leopard L1 with a Burlingham body dating from 1960. The operator is Stevenson's of Spath near Uttoxeter which was a family-owned business founded by John Stevenson in 1922. The company carried out various mergers and acquisitions in the 1980s and by the time it was purchased by British Bus in 1994 it was the largest independent operator in the UK, owning 270 buses, an accolade previously applying to Barton Transport. The vehicle shown here, Stevenson 18, was one of many second hand purchases, being acquired from Sheffield Joint Omnibus Committee in 1972 (their No 1307 and later 1007). The spacing of the registration number on the front seems somewhat odd. Other photographs of the bus show the registration correctly spaced as 5907 W. (Alan Murray-Rust/Online Transport Archive)

Greater Manchester Transport Daimler Fleetline No 6333 with East Lancs body leaves Bury Interchange to turn into Haymarket Street. This bus was formerly Bury Corporation 133 and entered service in 1965. It was subsumed into the newly created SELNEC on 1 November 1969 and this PTE was rebranded Greater Manchester Transport in 1974. The backdrop to this picture is now part of the Mill Gate shopping centre, with the towers having been retained. On the extreme left is the memorial to John Kay, inventor of a weaving machine, in front of which is a British Rail (BR) sign. The railway/bus interchange was opened by BR on 17 March 1980, the year in which this picture was taken and the Fleetline withdrawn. The replacement Metrolink to Bury did not arrive until 1991. I have never visited this facility myself but my late cousin, Victoria Wood, in statue form keeps an eye on it from a distance as she looks down Moss Street from her pedestal in Manchester Road. (Roy Marshall/The Bus Archive))

This rather haphazard bus station is beside the railway station in Station Terrace, Caerphilly, and was built on redundant railway land in 1973. It replaced a bus station round the corner in Mountain Road opposite the tall buildings in the centre background. The bus station pictured here in February 1976 was remodelled in 1999 to become Caerphilly Interchange with covered facilities for passengers transferring between road and rail, with buses parked in herringbone configuration. An attractive old style brick wall of medium height now separates the bus station from Station Terrace. The bus nearest the camera is Rhymney Valley District Council (RVDC) 15, a 1964 Leyland Leopard PSU3/1R in that municipality's brown, gold and cream livery. RVDC was formed in 1974 as an amalgamation of the urban district councils of Caerphilly, Bedwas & Machen and Gelligaer and their bus fleets were merged. When deregulation occurred in 1986 RVDC set up an arm's length separate bus company, Inter Valley Link, which the Council then sold to National Welsh three years later. (Alan Murray)

A protest march took place in a vain attempt to prevent Cambridge's Drummer Street bus station being built in 1925 on part of a public park called Christ's Pieces. Fast forward to 1991 when its modernisation eroded a little more of the park and generated more objections and even today the bus station creates controversy, with pressure mounting for it to be relocated. In this delightful sylvan setting ex-Ribble "White Lady" DCK 219, a Leyland PD2/3 Titan double deck coach with an East Lancs lowbridge body, has moved south along with other members of its type to join the fleet of Premier Travel of Cambridge, arriving in 1962. Today, this iconic vehicle is available for hire since joining the Stagecoach heritage fleet. The bus behind in this late 1960s view is Eastern Counties (ECOC) LM474, an ECW-bodied Bristol MW5G dating from 1963 which, like so many ECOC buses of the time, is just showing SERVICE as a destination. (John May/Online Transport Archive)

Above: Here is a bus station, located at Cannock in Staffordshire, which has not moved or been closed, and is still exposed to the elements although since this photograph was taken the stands have been totally reorganised. However, whether it survives a possible town centre regeneration initiative remains to be seen. The multi-storey car park in the background to which the clock tower is attached is under threat and has been closed since 2018 due to unsafe cladding but has been reprieved for the time being. The buses in this view are all carrying the livery of West Midlands PTE (WMPTE) which took over the municipal bus operations of Birmingham, Walsall, West Bromwich and Wolverhampton in 1969, with Coventry added in 1974. At the front of the queue is ex-Walsall Corporation 844, a Dennis Loline II which entered service in 1960. The third bus is WMPTE 4034, a Daimler Fleetline built in 1971. (Mike Russell)

Above right: Two buses wearing traditional deep red and cream livery feature in this picture taken in April 1968 at the East Kent Road Car Company's bus station at Canterbury. On the left is an AEC Reliance dating from 1967 standing beside a 1948 Dennis Lancet III. This was one of twenty-four from a batch of sixty rebuilt in 1959 with a forward entrance and full front in place of the original rear platform and half cab configuration to allow one-person operation (OPO). Canterbury bus station is still in situ but received a significant makeover in 2002. (Mike Russell)

Right: Still at Canterbury bus station, this picture was taken in December 1977 after East Kent's buses received NBC poppy red livery. On the left, in dual purpose livery, is Leyland National No 1082, just a few months old, and on the right is 1959 AEC Regent V PFN 874 which was bought for preservation in 1979 and now carries original livery. The Brutalist structure behind the Regent V is the staircase tower of a multi-storey car park opened in 1969 and demolished in 2001. The overall image of that part of St George's Lane overlooking the bus station is now much improved. (Chris Evans)

In the 1930s the old Great Western Railway complained to Cardiff Council about the view from the station which overlooked Temperance Town, a run-down residential area. The Council started protracted demolition in 1937 and the new Central bus station opposite the railway station opened in 1954. It was a huge facility with 34 stands and nothing much changed over subsequent years apart from the installation of domed shelters in 1982. That was until 2008 when the substantial brick building forming a familiar backdrop to so many photographs taken here was demolished, along with part of the bus station in 2008. The bus station eventually closed in 2015, with a replacement due to open on the site of the adjacent multi storey car park in 2023. In this early 1960s view, the front vehicle is Newport Corporation 163, a Leyland PD2/40 with a Longwell Green body dating from 1958. On the right is Red & White 3451, a 1953 Leyland Royal Tiger with a Lydney Coachworks body completed by Bristol Tramways' Body Building Works. Behind the PD2 is a Cardiff Corporation 1957 East Lancs-bodied Daimler CVG6. (John May/Online Transport Archive)

A queue of people prepares to board this 1964 Western SMT Alexander-bodied Leyland Leopard (No 1899) destined for Ecclefechan in Dumfries & Galloway. It is seen at Western's Carlisle bus station in the early 1970s. The Caledonian Omnibus Company built this combined bus garage and bus station in Lonsdale Street in 1937/8 which had separate entrance and exits between a two (later three) storey office block visible on the left. Meanwhile, Ribble built a separate bus station around the corner in Lowther Street. Western SMT acquired Caledonian in 1950 and took over the Lonsdale Street premises. These were closed in October 1981 and services were transferred to Lowther Street. Both bus station sites were redeveloped in the early 1990s for the Earls Lane shopping area as well as a new bus station which is accessed from Lonsdale Street. (W Ryan/Online Transport Archive)

Above left: Taking a liberal interpretation of the term "bus station", this bus lay-by on Mile End Road served Colchester North station. Colchester has a main bus station in the town centre (see next picture) but Colchester North was the principal railway station on the main line from London and is now simply called Colchester. However, it is located some distance from the town centre and bus connections have therefore always been important although the exact location shown here in 1964 is now untraceable. The bus in the foreground is former St Helens AEC Regent III No 70, a London Transport RT lookalike. St Helens withdrew the vehicle in 1962 and it was immediately purchased by Norfolk's of Nayland, Suffolk. This business started in 1868 and lasted until 1991 when it was bought by Hedingham & District Omnibuses. In the background is Colchester Corporation No 21, a 1959 Massey-bodied AEC Regent V which was renumbered 63 in 1973 and then withdrawn. (Marcus Eavis/Online Transport Archive)

Left: The bus station in Colchester town centre opened in the early 1960s as the Lewis Gardens bus station and was located in Queen Street. Originally open air, part of it was covered by a multi-storey car park in the early 1970s, as depicted here, but this was demolished in 1995 due to structural problems connected with the concrete used. The bus station returned to being open air and was upgraded in 2006. From 18 November 2012 it was replaced by on-street facilities in Osborne Street and Stanwell Street. This is designated as Colchester Bus Station on a building facade and some bus shelters and it does have a waiting room. Seen departing the Queens Street bus station in February 1980 is Hedingham & District L89, a Duple-bodied Bedford YLQ dating from 1978. The Company was formed in 1960 and operated until 2012 when it was bought by the Go Ahead Group. (Alan Murray)

Above: There is a profusion of Venture Transport vehicles in this view of the bus station in the former steel making town of Consett, Co Durham, but they would start to surrender their iconic livery to bland NBC poppy red from 1 May 1970. That was when Venture, a name carried by a horse-drawn coach used on the inaugural service between Shotley Bridge and Newcastle in 1891, was sold to Northern General, part of NBC. The Northern General vehicles in the picture are in pre-NBC livery. The bus station opened in 1936 and has undergone various modernisations since then but still occupies part of the original site. The vehicle in the foreground is an Alexander-bodied AEC Reliance from 1964 (Venture No 261) and is facing Victoria Road and the celebrated bus station clock. Following its removal the clock (or to be precise one that resembles it) has recently been reinstated. A car park adjacent to the Victoria Centre to the right of the buses now occupies a section of the bus station site. The buildings in the background in Medomsley Road are still standing. (Roy Marshall/The Bus Archive)

A bus station was first built on the green fields of Pool Meadow, Coventry, in 1931. It is still there today after undergoing various transformations, the latest one taking place in 1994 when the rows of bus shelters dating back to the early 1960s were finally replaced. This picture depicts Coventry Corporation No 42, a Daimler CVA6 of 1948 vintage against a backdrop which no longer exists. All the buildings have since been demolished including the large church (originally the Catholic Apostolic Church of St John's built in 1889) and the Art School. The section of Ford Street where they were located has disappeared. In the early 2000s there was even a risk of the bus station being closed due to access problems as a result of the revised road network but the problem was later overcome. (Ian Stewart/Online Transport Archive)

This 1970s view of Pool Meadow bus station depicts a Midland Red Fleetline, BMMO No 6006. This vehicle was built in 1966, converted to OPO in 1970 and withdrawn in 1979. Behind the Fleetline is the Ringway Viaduct carrying the Coventry Ring Road (A4053) built in the late 1960s. This road scheme and subsequent redevelopment in the area have resulted in the creation of new roads and the curtailment and realignment of other ones. Current pedestrian entrances to the bus station are imposing and resemble mini-Doric arches, one of which is beside the preserved Old Fire Station. However, the bus station is now nearly twenty years old and work has started on internal cosmetic improvements. (W Ryan/Online Transport Archive)

A group of waiting passengers gather in the bus shelter and one solitary soul sits in the waiting room at Darwen's bus station in August 1974. The sign on the shelter refers to two local Darwen roads, Chapels and Pothouse (short for Pot House Lane). The bus is former Darwen 32, a 1966 Leyland PD2A/27. The bus fleets of Darwen and Blackburn were merged on 1 April 1974 when the two boroughs amalgamated, with Blackburn taking precedence. Five months after the merger this PD2 is still in Darwen livery but has been renumbered 132. The building in the background is the Town Hall built in 1882 and the distant dome on the right belongs to Darwen Library which opened in 1908. Formerly called Darwen Circus, as stated on the bus blind, the area is now known as Market Place and has been mostly redeveloped into a landscaped open area which was completed in 2019. The bus station has shrunk and now consists of just two glazed bus shelters to the left of the picture. A huge statue of a peregrine falcon stands close to where the waiting room was located. (Mike Russell)

Derby's Art Deco Central Bus Station in Morledge opened in 1933 with curved platforms around a central hub. Unfortunately, in its later years it came to be regarded as not fit for purpose due to outmoded facilities and vehicle congestion. It was closed in October 2005 and demolished in the following year despite opposition from a protest group that hoisted a caravan onto one of the platform roofs and which was lived in for several weeks in a failed attempt to prevent destruction. The replacement bus station is roughly on the same site at Morledge/Cock Pitt and opened in March 2010. In this view from September 1982 the buildings visible consist of the Control Centre above the Derby Corporation Daimler Fleetline and the rear of the upper deck cafe on the far right. Facing forwards is Trent 563, an ECW-bodied Daimler Fleetline built in 1972. (Andrew Lowe)

The location of Dewsbury bus station in West Yorkshire as seen here is impossible to find today although its replacement which opened in 1979 is only a few hundred yards away. The old bus station was sandwiched between Vicarage Road and Longcauseway United Reformed church. The latter now stands beside the Princess of Wales shopping centre which has been built on the bus station site. The bus prominent in this view is Yorkshire Woollen District Transport 532, a Park Royal-bodied AEC Regent V originally delivered in 1964 to Sheffield Corporation which operated a "C fleet" on behalf of British Railways (fleet No C1151). On the right is Yorkshire Woollen 186, a Leyland Leopard from 1965. The building in the left background is the Bon Bon cafe situated in one of the roads which has disappeared as a result of the redevelopment. The cafe was attached to another building located roughly opposite the Minster Church of All Saints on the other side of Vicarage Road.

Around the time that Doncaster North bus station was built in 1967, there was a trend towards putting bus stations under new multi-storey car parks. This was seen as a cheap and convenient way of improving the lot of passengers by providing them with better protection rather than the previous rain swept facility, albeit now they would often be standing in a wind tunnel. Nowadays, with some towns abandoning bus stations altogether, the trend is to incorporate bus stations within commercial premises to help defray construction and running costs, although the downside from a passenger's point of view is that they tend to be gloomy places. Doncaster also boasted a South bus station which closed the day before the opening on 8 June 2006 of the new Frenchgate Interchange. This incorporates a shopping centre, Doncaster railway station and a bus station and is located close to the original North bus station. The latter closed on 18 March 2003 and was soon demolished along with the multi-storey car park. This scene from July 1983 depicts Yorkshire Traction 407, a 1973 Leyland National with a rebuilt front end, leaving the dark confines of the North bus station while South Yorkshire PTE's Leyland Fleetline No 1563 dating from 1976 catches the sunshine as a passenger prepares to board. (Mike Greenwood)

In 1934, Dundee Corporation opened the city's first bus station at Shore Terrace and this was followed in the following year by W Alexander & Sons of Falkirk opening their own bus station in Lindsay Street/South Ward Road. This was replaced in 1958 by the current bus station in Seagate, near the junction with Trades Lane, which came to be operated by Alexander Northern after W Alexander & Sons was divided into three separate companies covering their respective areas of operation. The bus station has since been rebuilt after this picture was taken in October 1976 and none of the buildings seen here survives. The bus featured is an Alexander-bodied Leyland PD3/3 which was new in 1958 and numbered RB 190 (later NRB 190). (Alan Murray-Rust/Online Transport Archive)

Until a new bus station opened in 1977 Durham had an ornate cast iron glazed bus station which was fine looking but draughty. When it was demolished Beamish Museum salvaged some components from the original structure (it was later extended) and has them stored for possible reuse in the long term. This view dates from July 1974 and depicts Northern General Routemaster No 2116 (3100 from 1975) which entered service in January 1965 and was withdrawn in October 1980, whereupon it was scrapped. On the left is a 1961 United Automobile Services Bristol MW5G with ECW bodywork in pre-NBC livery. This was originally Durham District Services DBE17 and would have carried green and cream livery. This company comprising three former independents was formed in 1950 by the British Transport Commission and managed by United until taken over by United in 1968. (Charles Dean/Kevin Lane collection)

Above: Unlike cities such as Glasgow, Edinburgh just had one central bus station. Buses terminated around St Andrew Square until the bus station opened in April 1957. A road ran through the middle of it (Clyde Street), with Stances A-D on one side and Stance E on the other side. All the buildings on the left (in Clyde Street) and at the back (in Elder Street) have been demolished. In this early 1960s view the bus approaching the photographer in Scottish Motor Traction (SMT) livery is Scottish Omnibus D2 which was withdrawn in 1962. This vehicle was originally London Transport (LT) austerity double-deck Guy Arab II No G204 which was bought by Scottish Omnibuses in 1951 and rebodied as a single decker in 1954. Waiting at Stance B is Scottish Omnibuses BB79, a 1949 AEC Regent III with a Duple lowbridge body. (Ian Dunnet/Online Transport Archive)

Above right: Long distance bus services and coach tours occupied Stance E at St Andrew Square bus station, Edinburgh, and in the foreground is an ECW-bodied Bristol LS6G delivered to Scottish Omnibuses in 1956 (No A46) and carrying the Eastern Scottish fleetname. Standing alongside is Eastern Scottish Alexander-bodied Bristol RELH6G, No YA 196. The Eastern Scottish enquiries entrance visible in the picture is on the corner of North Clyde Street Lane. Part of this lane still exists running alongside, and then truncated, by the new Edinburgh bus station. The new bus station which opened in 2003 is built close to the site of the old Stance E and is accessed by buses from Elder Street, just as before. The buildings seen here have all been demolished, making way for a major redevelopment, but those on the far left which stand in York Place are still in situ. (Ian Dunnet/Online Transport Archive)

Right: The open aspect of St Andrew Square bus station was lost in the 1970s when it became partially enveloped by office blocks. Only the concrete shelter on the left provides an indication that this is the same location as the first picture. This depressing version of the bus station closed in 2000 and the adjoining St James shopping centre completed in 1973, which could be accessed from nearby Elder Street, closed in 2016 and has also been demolished. The buses seen here both belong to Scottish Omnibus and are No AA216, a Bristol Lodekka from 1966, and No ZS918, an Alexander-bodied Seddon Pennine 7 delivered in 1979. (W Ryan /Online Transport Archive)

Evesham in Worcestershire possesses, according to current timetables, a bus station but this is a somewhat liberal interpretation of the term since it consists of just a few bus stops and shelters alongside the pavement on both sides of the High Street. Previously, the buses were still parked in the same spot but at least in a bus station type formation, as evidenced in this view of eight Midland Red buses. They are facing south west but in Midland Red West days an arrangement was created for buses to be off the road with loading bays facing north. Where the buses are standing is now a wide pedestrian zone running parallel with the High Street. All the buildings behind the buses are still standing (the one with the small white gable is The Olde Swanne Inne) but the large Victorian edifice in the left background has been replaced. The vehicles are all built and owned by the Birmingham & Midland Motor Omnibus Company (BMMO) which used the fleet name Midland but was better known as Midland Red. This latter name was applied to newer buses from 1968 and on all buses from 1970, having originally been adopted on new coaches in the late 1950s. (Geoff Morant)

This is another view of Folkestone bus station (see front cover) looking in the opposite direction. All the buildings creating the backdrop to this picture taken in July 1961 have been demolished. The Bouverie Place shopping centre now stands alongside the bus station. The vehicle nearest the camera is East Kent CJG 977, a lowbridge Leyland PD1 built in 1948, beside which is a lowbridge Park Royal-bodied Guy Arab dating from 1950, EFN 184. Alongside the latter is a Maidstone & District vehicle on the joint East Kent/M&D Service 10 between Folkestone and Maidstone via Ashford. East Kent buses were not allotted fleet numbers until 1978. The Canterbury-based East Kent Road Car Company was formed in 1916 and became part of NBC in 1969. It was acquired by Stagecoach in 1993. (C Carter/Online Transport Archive)

Several bus garages doubled as bus stations and one such example was Ribble's outstation at Garstang in Lancashire, between Preston and Lancaster. Generally, local services and northbound ones reversed into the depot to take on passengers while southbound services left from the forecourt. In this view groups of people are standing around in the absence of a waiting room but there were some facilities available as evidenced here by the snack and milk machines as well as the toilets just inside the entrance. The bus facing north on the forecourt is Ribble 1622, a Leyland PDR1/1 Atlantean built in 1959. Today, there is no evidence of the depot/bus station ever having existed. The site in Bridge Street is now occupied by housing although the buildings in front of the bus are still extant. (W Ryan/Online Transport Archive)

For many years Glasgow had a scattering of smaller bus stations rather than one large central one: Waterloo Street, Blythwood Street (Anderston Cross), Killermont Street (Buchanan Street) and Dundas Street. This is the last mentioned one, seen against the backdrop of Parliamentary Road, hence the aptly named Parly Road Cafe. Also in view is the Lemon Tree pub at 394 Parliamentary Road on the corner of Pladda Street which was demolished in 1964 and was so named by the last proprietor, Richard Lemon. In fact, all the buildings in this picture have been demolished and roads removed or realigned as part of the slum clearance and redevelopment which followed the closure and removal of nearby Buchanan Street station in the late 1960s. The bus, a Bristol Lodekka new to David Lawson of Kirkintilloch in 1956 (No RD16), is in their livery This company was taken over by W Alexander and Sons in 1936 but became a subsidiary, retaining its own identity until the splitting of Alexander into three companies in 1961. (Ian Stewart/Online Transport Archive)

This is Buchanan bus station in Glasgow which is officially located in Killermont Street, a road which has been realigned and bears no resemblance to the previous one despite being in the same area. The bus station opened in 1977 and part of it was built on the old Buchanan Street goods depot site. In fact, it is situated very close to the locations of the old Killermont and Dundas Street bus stations which were closed in anticipation of the new one being built. This picture was taken soon after the bus station opened and depicts Alexander Midland and Eastern Scottish vehicles. The departing bus is an Alexander-bodied Daimler Fleetline, No MRF 19, delivered to Alexander Midland in 1967. The body building side of W Alexander & Sons was put into a separate company following the 1947 Transport Act to retain its independence and prevent it from being nationalised. (W Ryan/Online Transport Archive)

Viewed in August 1985 over stances 48-57, Buchanan bus station has a completely different backdrop from the one in the previous picture taken less than ten years earlier. Tower blocks of flats have risen but the low level residential buildings in St Mungo Avenue remain although nowadays they have gabled roofs. The bus station lies between Cowcaddens Road on the left (bordered by stances 1-22), the realigned Killermont Street on the right (stances 33-47) and North Hanover Street (stances 23-32) beyond the buses. Until 1993, the bus station was owned by the Scottish Bus Group whose subsidiaries, restructured and renamed in June 1985 in preparation for deregulation and privatisation, operate the service buses seen here: red Central Scottish (ex-Central SMT), blue Midland Scottish (ex-Alexander (Midland) and green Eastern Scottish (same branding as previously). The yellow and two-tone blue livery belongs to Scottish Citylink. The Routemaster (RM 652), which has just negotiated the patched –up disintegrating concrete surface, is still in LT livery. It was on trial for Clydeside Scottish and purchased in the following month. Following withdrawal it spent a period in preservation before returning to London and re-entering service, being used on heritage route 15. (Gavin Booth)

There is still a bus station at the Gosport Ferry Terminal (where a four-minute sea trip to Portsmouth is available) but it is a little smaller. Buses no longer face the shops and flats in South Street which are still in situ. Gosport Ferry was the hub for services operated by the Gosport and Fareham Omnibus Company, a subsidiary of the Provincial Traction Company, and was noted for its elderly vehicles, albeit most were given replacement bodies. This view from September 1968 depicts No 27, an AEC Regal 1 from 1934 which was rebodied in 1961 and still carries the Company's garter crest and Provincial fleetname in script. (W Ryan/Online Transport Archive)

Also seen at Gosport Ferry, this time in August 1970, is another old stager, chassis-wise and one which again is wearing the Provincial name in script. This is Guy Arab II, No 57, from 1943 which was rebodied in 1953, withdrawn in October 1970 and is now preserved. The disinterested dog on the left is waiting to board one of Provincial's first OPO vehicles, a Sedden Pennine built in 1968 (No 42). Provincial was sold in 1969 to the Wiles/Swain Group and its bus operations were subsumed by NBC on 1 January 1970 and administered by Hants & Dorset Motor Services. (Mike Russell)

Until Guildford's Friary bus station opened in November 1980 (a station now regarded as outdated and destined for replacement) the town boasted two bus stations created in 1949/50 on opposite sides of the River Wey and both were used by the major operators: Aldershot & District, London Transport, Tillingbourne Valley and Safeguard. Only the last-named family-owned business still provides bus services in Guildford which it has been doing since 1924. This photograph depicts Farnham Road bus station, now used as a car park, with Aldershot & District 131, a 1949 East Lancs-bodied Dennis Lance K3, occupying centre stage while a Lance K4, No 217, stands in the background. (Phil Tatt/Online Transport Archive)

All the aforementioned operators feature in this picture at Farnham Road taken in May 1968. From left to right the vehicles are A&D's AEC Reliance No 292 from 1957, a Safeguard AEC Reliance, Tillingbourne's ex-LT GS 4 and LT's RF 599 working route 432. Tillingbourne and LT jointly operated a 448 service until LT pulled out in 1964. Tillingbourne went on to buy thirteen of LT's GS buses for use on various routes. The Company folded in 2001. Farnham Road is one of the sites being considered for the proposed replacement for the Friary bus station. (W Ryan/Online Transport Archive)

Diagonally opposite and visible from Guildford's Farnham Road bus station was Onslow Street bus station depicted in this scene. Like Farnham Road, it closed in November 1980 upon the opening of the Friary bus station. Another factor which they both have in common is that, despite the passage of time (some forty years), neither site has been built on. Onslow Street station has become an open area in front of the Electric Theatre which incorporates the former Electricity Works of 1913 that forms the backdrop to many bus photographs taken here. It doesn't feature in this view and neither does another familiar backdrop: the Rodboro Buildings (now a pub) which is where the Dennis Brothers started their bus building business in the 1900s. In this view from May 1968 A&D 443, an Alexander-bodied Dennis Loline III dating from 1962, lays over. Another one stands in the background. No 443 was transferred to Alder Valley on 1 January 1972, becoming their No 785. (W Ryan/Online Transport Archive)

A large number of passengers are milling about in this view of Onslow Street bus station also dating from May 1968. Here we have two LT services being operated by vehicles based at Guildford bus garage. These are RT 4755 and lowbridge RLH 25, the one foot difference in height being instantly evident. The RT is working a short local route which justifies its "lazy" blind. The RLH has no rear blind aperture, nor does the stencil frame on the staircase lower window contain a route number stencil plate, a practice discontinued by this time. RT 4755 dates from 1954 but was stored for some four years before entering service. It was transferred to London Country Bus Services (LCBS) on 1 January 1970 and withdrawn in 1976, followed by scrapping. RLH 25 entered service in 1952 and was also transferred to LCBS but lasted only a few months.Following withdrawal in July1970, it was exported to the USA in 1973. (W Ryan/Online Transport Archive)

Above left: Standing in Cross Field bus station, Halifax, are two Yorkshire Woollen District buses. In the foreground is No 570, a former Leyland PS1 single decker from 1947 rebodied as a double decker by Metro-Cammell in 1954/5. Behind is No 720, a 1950 Leyland PS2 with a Willowbrook body carrying OPO/summer touring livery. The building of the bus station was proposed in 1936 but it did not open until August 1954 following housing demolition on the site, with further redevelopment of the area continuing through the remainder of the century. The bus station had five loading platforms and the buses seen here are at platform D which was for Yorkshire Woollen services. The passengers behind No 570 are waiting for Hebble services on Platform E, adjacent to Great Albion Street. The large building in the background is the Odd Fellows Hall in St James's Road which later became the Alhambra cinema and was demolished in 1963. Cross Field station closed in October 1993 after a new one had opened in Winding Road in 1989. This is now scheduled to be replaced. (Phil Tatt/ Online Transport Archive)

Left: It is all change at Hanley bus station since this photograph was taken. The station in Lichfield Street seen here was built together with the adjacent East-West shopping centre in the mid 1960s. It was demolished in 2019 but had already been replaced in 2013 by a new bus station slightly further along Lichfield Street built on the site of the former John Street car park. The new Hanley bus station is officially called Stoke-on-Trent City Centre Bus Station. Hanley was one of six towns merged into the county borough of Stoke-on-Trent in 1910 and is generally regarded as constituting the city centre. The ornate building in the background is Hanley swimming baths in Lichfield Street which opened in 1873 and was demolished in 1981. In this view from April 1968, Massey-bodied Leyland PD3/1 No 12 built in 1959 is backing off the stand. The operator is S Turner & Sons of Brown Edge, a village some five miles from Hanley. Sammy Turner started this independent business in 1921 and the company was sold to Potteries Motor Traction (PMT) in 1987. (W Ryan/Online Transport Archive)

Above: In today's age of transport hubs, Harrogate bus station was something of a pioneer, being built alongside the town's railway station. In this early 1970s view, the West Yorkshire Road Car Company is seen to have proudly displayed its name on the frontage. The strange looking protuberance on the roof at the far end is the reverse of a bus station sign. A new bus station in Station Parade on the site of the one shown here was opened in September 2002 and has normal modern pull-in, reverse-out bays. The shelter for passengers is of retrospective appearance and has glass panels on the pavement side, otherwise it would be very draughty. West Yorkshire received its name in 1927 following a merger and became part of NBC in 1969. The vehicle shown here is West Yorkshire VR 48 (renumbered to 1948 in 1971), an ECW-bodied Bristol VRT built in late 1969. (John May/Online Transport Archive)

This is Heworth Metro Interchange in Gateshead, some three miles from Newcastle-upon-Tyne on the other side of the river. The bus station is complementary to the adjacent railway station used by the Tyne and Wear Metro light rail system and Network Rail services. The bus station opened in November 1979 when the Haymarket – Heworth section of the Metro came into operation and was refurbished in November 2012. The three buses seen here in March 1982 are all destined for South Shields as the opening of the Metro from Heworth to South Shields did not occur until March 1984. The two buses at the front are, from left to right, Northern General Transport (NGT) 3450 and 3468, both Roe-bodied Leyland AN68 Atlanteans built in 1980. They are in yellow rather than NGT red livery for operation within the Tyne & Wear PTE area. The bus behind is Tyne & Wear PTE 348, an Alexander-bodied Leyland AN68 Atlantean dating from 1973. (Charles Roberts/Online Transport Archive)

Standing on the site of the former District Railway Hounslow Town station, Hounslow bus station was created in 1954 on the corner of London Road and Kingsley Road alongside the bus garage and is still in situ today. However, it has since lost its canopy which was fitted in 1970 and its islands have been reduced in number following widening. In this scene from May 1972 during the period when suburban crew working was being phased out, a variety of LT bus types are on display: three Swifts, two Routemasters, an RF and an RT. From right to left the nearest four vehicles are RM 1094 (sold for scrap in 1987), RF 522 (originally RF 303, bought for spares in 1998), SMS 232 (exported to Malta in 1981) and RM 1134 (which went to Baghdad in 1993 on a fund raising mission). (Author)

This is the old Hull Coach Station in Collier Street built in 1935 beside Hull Paragon railway station, visible in the background. This so-called coach station, intended to convey an illusion of superiority over a bus station, was used by Kingston upon Hull Corporation Transport for its bus services, as evidenced here. It was superseded by Hull Paragon Interchange which opened in 2007 and is similarly adjacent to the railway station. Hull is the name of the river on which the port stands and is a popular abbreviation for the city of Kingston upon Hull. During the 1960s Hull Corporation purchased a large number of second-hand buses as a stopgap to cover the transition from old bus types to OPO vehicles such as those in the background of this picture. In the foreground is Park Royal-bodied AEC Regent III No 158 built in 1953 and originally delivered to Nottingham Corporation along with 71 other such vehicles. Hull bought half the fleet in 1967 and operated them until the start of the 1970s. (David Christie)

Hyde, in Tameside, Greater Manchester, followed the normal Manchester area bus station design with individual shelters. These were made of concrete and served the ten stands but were replaced by more modern ones in 1977. The bus station was completely reconstructed in 2007 with an island covered waiting area for passengers but the number of stands was reduced to six. In this c.1969/70 view the buses are all carrying their traditional Corporation liveries and pre-SELNEC numbers. On the left is Stockport No 347, a Leyland PD2/30 with Longwell Green body dating from 1960 and in the centre, also in Stockport livery, is former No 297, an all Leyland PD 2/1 which was new in 1951 but has been allocated No 51 in the fleet of SHMD following transfer to SELNEC. SHMD were the initials of the Stalybridge, Hyde, Mossley & Dukinfield Joint Transport & Electricity Board whose livery is carried by the vehicle on the right, No 83, a 1957 Daimler CVG6 with Northern Counties bodywork. In the distance is a Daimler Fleetline, also with Northern Counties bodywork, new to SHMD.
(Howard J Piltz/Online Transport Archive)

Not many towns can boast two bus stations but Ipswich can. One is Tower Ramparts bus station pictured here, built on a former car park and renovated in 2013. On the far left is the Cricketers pub in Crown Street, the design of which was inspired by Helmingham Hall in Suffolk. Until their withdrawal in 1963, trolleybuses used to terminate here along the road called Tower Ramparts, this part having since been incorporated into the bus station. The trolleybuses used to show Electric House as the destination on their blinds, as do the buses in this photograph. Electric House is a well known Art Deco building dating from 1933 located in Lloyds Avenue and faces the bus station. In this view the buses are Borough of Ipswich Nos 18 and 90. The first is a Roe-bodied Leyland Atlantean built in 1976 and the second is an AEC Swift dating from 1973 and withdrawn in 1986. This was the same year that the Borough Council had to transfer its assets into a separate legal entity. Currently branded Ipswich Buses, this company remains wholly owned by the Council. (Geoff Morant)

Whereas the last picture depicted the Crown Street side of the bus station, this is the Tower Ramparts side featuring two East Lancs-bodied AEC Swifts built in 1973, No 90 which also appears on the previous page and No 93. This view was taken in July 1984 and the buses are carrying signs on the front stating "Welcome to Floral Ipswich". Tower Ramparts serves the Council's town routes while the second one, Old Cattle Market bus station, was the former Eastern Counties facility and serves the out of town routes. On the right of the picture, following the demolition of Tower Ramparts school in 1979, the Tower Ramparts shopping centre development is under way. This opened in 1986 and since being revamped has been renamed Sailmakers shopping centre. (John Bath)

School children scramble aboard Cumberland Motor Services 256, an ECW-bodied Bristol RELL6L built in 1967. The location is Keswick bus station, which opened in June 1933, and the picture was taken around 1970, just after Cumberland Motor Services (CMS) had become a subsidiary of NBC. On the extreme left is the corner of Cumberland's Keswick garage which was later swept away together with the bus station. There is no trace of this site today but a clue to its location remains: the unusual style of half timbering on the gable end of the building in the distance. This is the Crosthwaite Parish Room in Main Street. Keswick's transport hub is now centred on three exposed bus stops at the junction of Elliot Park and the Headlands outside Booth's supermarket. Bus shelters are not provided so passengers have to use the supermarket entrance canopy in inclement weather. (W Ryan/Online Transport Archive)

Keswick bus station could become congested at times and there was an overflow area with platforms and shelters situated opposite. In this mid-1960s view prior to the NBC takeover, three CMS Bristol buses stand ready for service. From left to right these are Bristol LD6G Lodekka No 354 built in 1955, FLF6G No 532 dating from1965 and MW6G No 228. This latter vehicle entered service in 1962 as No 427 and its fleet number was changed to 228 in April 1964. The origin of CMS can be traced back to October1912 when a new company called Whitehaven Motor Services started its first regular bus service, and this operator changing its name to Cumberland Motor Services in June 1921. When NBC was disbanded in preparation for deregulation, CMS had become its most profitable company despite the relatively sparse population which it served. (John May/Online Transport Archive)

Like Keswick and several other towns, Kettering has lost its bus station in favour of street stops with minimal facilities for passengers. Plans for a bus station were made in 1935 when United Counties built their garage in Northampton Road, near the junction with Sheep Street. This remains in place and now belongs to Stagecoach but there is very little trace of the bus station built alongside the garage. World War II delayed its construction and opening did not occur until July 1963. The bus station was well appointed, with toilets, cafeteria, waiting room and travel shop. Following closure in 1986, a block of flats now stands in its place. Substitute bus shelters and rows of bus stops have been provided in Newland Street and adjacent Eskdaill Street. Leaving the bus station in this view is United Counties No 198, a Leyland Tiger Cub PSUC1/2 with Metro-Cammell bodywork built in 1960 for East Yorkshire (No 685). It was purchased by United Counties in May 1972. The tall building at the rear of the bus is part of the former George/Naseby Hotel dating from 1766 and survives on the corner of George Street and Oak Tree Court. (Alan Murray-Rust/Online Transport Archive)

This is the same bus station at Kettering but showing a different perspective, with buses entering from George Street. The houses remain today but the building on the right has been redeveloped. The buses, which are standing in what is now the entrance to Oak Tree Court, are United Counties Bristol VRTs. On the left and carrying a special United Counties 60th Anniversary livery (1921-1981) is No 834 which entered service in 1975. Alongside, in normal United Counties colours for this period (NBC leaf green) is No 912 dating from 1979. In 1921 United Counties Omnibus and Road Transport Company purchased the assets of Wellingborough Motor Omnibus Company which began operating in 1913. The Road Transport part of the name was removed in 1933. Following the breaking up of NBC in preparation for deregulation, United Counties was acquired by Stagecoach in November 1987. (Alan Murray-Rust/Online Transport Archive)

Built in 1924, this distinctive bus station in Portland Street served Kilmarnock, East Ayrshire, until the 1970s when it was demolished along with the building next to it. The area is now a surface car park. The building on the far left has survived as indeed has the "bridge". This is actually a 23-arch viaduct completed in 1850 which carries the Glasgow to Carlisle railway line. The bus in the foreground is Western SMT 1216, a 1956 Leyland PD2/20 with a Northern Counties lowbridge body. Beyond is a 1959 Leyland PD3/3 with an Alexander lowbridge body. In addition to the Western SMT bus station, Kilmarnock boasted a second one from 1959. This belonged to Ayrshire Bus Owners (A1 Services) Ltd located in John Dickie Street. Both were replaced by the current one in Green Street. (Geoff Pullin/Online Transport Archive)

Kirkcaldy had a windswept bus station at the Esplanade which closed in the 1980s and this one in the town centre, located in Hunter Place, which is still extant, albeit somewhat modernised. The stone wall behind the buses has made way for the Postings shopping centre and where the people are seated on the right is now the location of the bus station building. The backdrop of chimney stacks remains as does the rounded building (now belonging to the Salvation Army) in Hill Street but only the very top is visible from the photographer's position. The three buses are sporting the old W Alexander & Sons fleet name prior to the formation of Alexander Fife in 1961 and are not in the traditional blue livery because the buses serving Perth City and Kirkcaldy town services were painted deep red, a brighter shade of red being subsequently adopted by Alexander Fife. The bus on the left is an ECW-bodied Bristol Lodekka from 1959 (No RD79) and the other two are 1944 Guy Arab IIs which have retained their Roe and Northern Counties wartime utility bodies. (Ian Dunnet/Online Transport Archive)

There has been a bus station at Cable Street, Lancaster, since 1939, and, after various modernisation schemes over the years, the latest manifestation opened in 2001 on the same site. Buses enter from Damside Street and exit into Cable Street. This view captures ex-Morecambe & Heysham 73, a 1951 AEC Regent III with a typical "flaired skirt" Weymann body and now preserved in working order. Local government reorganisation in 1974 brought about the amalgamation of Morecambe & Heysham and Lancaster councils and the bus fleets were merged. Lancaster's ruby and broken white livery and Morecambe & Heysham's green and cream (carried by No 73 today) were discontinued and a new livery of Trafalgar blue and white was introduced, as displayed here on No 73 while on learner duties. This was the only closed top Regent III to receive blue livery and a unique fleetname style. In the late 1970s the No Entry signs were removed and buses loaded up on both sides of this roadway in the bus station. The spire in the background belongs to St John the Evangelist's church in North Road which still stands, as does the gabled building behind the bus. (W Ryan/Online Transport Archive)

A variety of buses populate Lancaster bus station in this 1979 scene, most of them belonging to Ribble. However, the foreground is taken by Lancaster City Council 204, an East Lancs-bodied Leyland PD2/37 delivered in 1965 and withdrawn in 1980. A working after-life then ensued for this vehicle with various owners, including Northern General which used it for training purposes (No T591) in the mid 1980s. It is now part of the Ensignbus Hire Fleet and has been returned to its original Lancaster ruby and broken white livery. Much of the area around the bus station consists of historic buildings but the one in Damside Street visible in this photograph was clearly not regarded as worthy of retention and has been replaced. (W Ryan/Online Transport Archive)

Today's Leeds City Bus Station now stands on the site of the 1938 Leeds Central Bus station seen here in August 1959. The iconic Quarry Hill flats on the right, containing 938 flats housing some 3000 people, were also built in 1938 and demolished in 1978. This photograph was taken from a section of the railway embankment within a public area overlooking York Street. This scene is now totally unrecognisable apart from the grass and the two round top pillars (one shorter than the other) in the foreground. Central Bus Station was known locally as the "green bus station" as it was used by the Corporation fleet and West Riding which carried green livery in order to distinguish it from the "red bus station" in Vicar Lane belonging to West Yorkshire Road Car Company whose buses were red. Central bus station was remodelled in 1964 with curved platforms and shelters and then totally rebuilt in the 1990s, becoming Leeds City Bus Station when it reopened in 1996. Further modernisation is now planned. In the centre of this picture is an ex-London Transport Feltham tram which became Leeds No 538. The tram system closed in November 1959. (Marcus Eavis/Online Transport Archive)

Leek bus station in Staffordshire was built as part of the Smithfield Shopping Centre in 1963 on the site of the former cattle market. However, there have been complaints recently that the bus station is outdated and grim. In 2018/9 the local District Council implemented some improvements by resurfacing the road outside (Cromwell Terrace) and refurbishing the toilets but some of the original passenger amenities have been permanently closed. The Waiting Room has been bricked up and a false teeth emporium now occupies the former Booking and Enquiries Office outside Stand 2 on the far left of this early 1970s picture. The distinctive vehicle at Stand 3 is a third-hand purchase by Berresford of Cheddleton, near Leek. Entering service with Silver Star of Porton Down in 1957 this Harrington-bodied Leyland Tiger Cub later became Wilts & Dorset 905 following the latter's acquisition of Silver Star in 1963 before joining the Berresford fleet. The vehicle in front is Proctor's Daimler Fleetline 4559 VC. (W Ryan/Online Transport Archive)

Above left: This version of Leicester's St Margarets Bus Station was opened in 1941 and was noted for its rows of utilitarian concrete bus shelters, a consequence of wartime privations. It is perhaps surprising that it lasted until 1984. All the buildings in the background in Abbey Street are still extant at the time of writing but the bus would now be standing in Gravel Street which ran alongside the 1980s replacement bus station main building. In this photograph taken in May 1981, the vehicle at Stand 3 is BMMO 6428, a Willowbrook-bodied Leyland Leopard dating from 1971 and withdrawn in 1983. (Charles Roberts/Online Transport Archive)

Left: Photographed in May 1985 just after it opened in Leicester, this is the replacement bus station for the 1941 version and yet today it is already obsolete despite its relatively modern appearance. It closed on 31 December 2020 and construction of an even newer bus station started in 2021 in the same place. This latest manifestation is intended to be the UK's first carbon neutral bus station. The two double deckers on the left are worth a mention because they are second hand, being ex-London Transport Daimler Fleetlines. The vehicle in red, white and yellow livery advertising National Holidays is former DM 1772 which entered LT service in January 1975 and was sold in 1982 to Midland Red East which changed its name to Midland Fox in January 1984. The bus was withdrawn in 1991 and scrapped. The second Fleetline is ex-DM 1735 from 1974 which was bought by Midland Red East/Midland Fox in 1983. It too was withdrawn in 1991 and sold for scrap. (Mike Greenwood)

Above: Despite carrying its new SELNEC 6954 number, this vehicle is still wearing its former Leigh Corporation livery as it stands at Leigh bus station, Greater Manchester. All Leigh Corporation double deckers were lowbridge because of the headroom in the depot and this example, originally No 54, is a Leyland PD2/20 with East Lancs body delivered in 1957. Leigh Corporation began bus operations in 1920 and these ended on 1 November 1969 when the fleet was absorbed into SELNEC. Leigh originally had two small bus stations in King Street and Spinning Jenny Street. The latter, used by Lancashire United, opened in 1927 and was the terminus for trolleybus services to Bolton and Moseley Common. Leigh Corporation constructed its own station at King Street which opened in May 1955. In 1991 this site was used to construct a new combined bus station, resulting in the closure of Spinning Jenny Street and the demolition of the Woolpack pub in King Street. A further refurbishment of King Street took place in 2015. All the buildings in the background of this picture have been replaced. (W Ryan/Online Transport Archive)

Above: Visiting Lichfield bus station today is like entering a time warp because its appearance has hardly changed from June 1967 when this picture was taken except that the Kenning Motors building behind the bus has been demolished, albeit only recently, and the area to the right is no longer used by buses. It could be regarded as an early interchange as the railway station is virtually opposite, although access requires crossing the A5127 Birmingham Road. The bus, a Leyland OPD 2/1 originally intended for export, has an interesting history because it was delivered as a Weymann-bodied single decker in 1950 to PMT, becoming No 448. In 1955 it became H448 and was fitted with a Northern Counties double deck second hand body built in 1951 which was previously carried by TD4 Reg No CVT 9. In this picture the bus, No 33, is operating for Whieldon of Rugeley trading as Green Bus, a family business which started bus operation in 1927 and was bought out by BMMO (Midland Red) in November 1973. PMT had twenty-four of these rebodied buses and a similar highbridge one, No L453, is preserved and operational. (W Ryan/Online Transport Archive)

Below left: Against the backdrop of two of "The Three Graces" on Liverpool's River Mersey waterfront (the Cunard Building and the Port of Liverpool Building), a group of Liverpool City Transport buses stand at Pier Head bus station in January 1969. The radiator is being topped-up on L201, a Weymann-bodied Leyland PD2/20 dating from 1955 and on the left is L79, another PD2/20, this time with Alexander bodywork and in reversed livery of mainly cream for the City Circle. The bus station opened on 11 April 1965, replacing stops for terminating buses around the perimeter of the former tram loops. It was closed in 1991 and demolished because there was no need for a large bus station at Pier Head due to declining numbers of office workers and Wallasey ferry commuters. The pattern of bus routes was accordingly reorganised to compensate. In addition, there used to be a small Central bus station which closed when a new one was opened in November 2005 as part of the Liverpool One development. (W Ryan/Online Transport Archive)

A different perspective of Pier Head bus station is provided by this 1982 view from another of "The Three Graces", the Royal Liver Building. The previous picture was taken from the opposite direction, with the cameraman positioned in the right hand upper corner where the three buses are standing, looking towards the two buses parked one behind the other close to the all-over advertising one in the same place as the PD2s. By now all the vehicles, mainly Leyland Atlanteans and Scania Metropolitans, are in Merseyside PTE livery. The ship with the bunting is the Isle of Man Steam Packet Company's *Manxman*, a turbine steam ship launched in 1955 and seen here in its last year of service. It then served as a floating night club in Preston and later in Liverpool. Following a fire it was towed to Sunderland in 1997 but after a failed preservation scheme it was broken up in 2012. (Roger Barton)

Departing from Longton bus station, Stoke on Trent, in August 1974 is Berresford lowbridge Leyland Atlantean, 1013 MW. This PMT combined depot and bus station in Commerce Street superseded a traditional exposed bus station but was itself replaced by Longton Transport Interchange in Baths Road which opened in 2003. Over the years various businesses occupied the area above the bus station including a combined restaurant/bowling alley and a cabaret club. The building was reconstructed in 2004 using the original framework and the section seen here is now a branch of Wilco. Berresford Motors of Cheddleton was taken over by PMT in 1987 but 1013 MW lives on in preservation. Originally No 42 in the fleet of Silver Star of Porton Down when built in 1962 it was purchased by Bristol Omnibus in 1963 and had its iconic Silver Star front roof box removed (now reinstated). Following purchase by Super Coaches of Upminster, the bus was then acquired by Berresford in 1967. The other bus featured in the picture is PMT 196, a 1972 Bristol RESL. Longton was another of the six towns which amalgamated to form the County Borough of Stoke on Trent in 1910. (Mike Russell)

In High Street, Lymington, in the New Forest, there was a gap between numbers 35 and 36, which was the entrance to the bus station pictured here in August 1974. The bus station closed in 2015 and was sold by Go Ahead. It was then used for bus storage while various development proposals were submitted to the Council and rejected. In 2019 a scheme was accepted and demolition of the bus station took place. It has not been replaced because the bus operator, in the light of reduced Council subsidies, decided to make savings by selling infrastructure instead of cutting services. In this view, Hants & Dorset 1440, a Bristol FS6B Lodekka with ECW bodywork, still in Tilling green and cream but with an NBC style fleetname, fills up with passengers before setting off for Bournemouth. (Mike Greenwood)

Above left: This is the former North Western Road Car Company bus station in Sunderland Street, Macclesfield seen in 1976. The station opened in September 1939 alongside North Western's depot which had opened six months earlier. After the Company became part of NBC its depots were split between SELNEC and Crosville in 1972, Macclesfield depot passing to Crosville. The garage is on the far right of the picture. The Sunderland Road bus station was replaced by a new one in Mill Street in 2003 and following the closure of the garage in the following year the site was redeveloped. In this view the bus nearest the camera is Crosville EMG 483, a Bristol MW6G built in 1963 with ECW bodywork and numbered CMG 483 until 1975. It was withdrawn in 1977. On its left is Crosville Leyland National ENL 862 dating from 1974. (W Ryan/Online Transport Archive).

Left: Maesteg bus station near Bridgend, South Wales, looks especially uninviting in this April 1979 view. However, it has since received a minor makeover with the provision of shelters and six proper bus stands located on the right hand side next to the covered waiting area. The facility is in Church Street directly behind the Town Hall and the buildings which make up the backdrop remain in situ apart from the fire station and its training tower on the left which have been demolished. The pale blue buses belong to Brewer's Motor Services of Caerau which became part of the United Welsh Group in 1988, having first been acquired by, but not absorbed by South Wales Transport. Also in 1988 Brewer's acquired Llynfi Motor Services of Maesteg, the operator of the dark blue bus in the centre. This vehicle is a Leyland Leopard PSU3/1 with a Weymann body delivered new to County Motors (Lepton) in 1965 and becoming Yorkshire Traction 395 three years later. On the right is former City of Cardiff Transport 518, an Alexander-bodied 1968 AEC Swift. (Alan Murray-Rust/Online Transport Archive)

Above: Lower Mosley Street bus station in Manchester opened in 1928 adjacent to Manchester Central railway station which was situated across the road to the left of the white bus station building in the photograph. It was mainly used for longer distance and express services including those serving holiday destinations and consequently could become very busy on summer Saturdays. This view dates from April 1967 and depicts East Lancs-bodied North Western 818, a Dennis Loline II built in 1960, about to turn into Great Bridgewater Street and squeezing between Lancashire United 91, a 1962 Plaxton-bodied AEC Reliance coach, and North Western 579, a Weymann-bodied Leyland Tiger Cub from 1955. The bus station closed when the last bus departed on 13 May 1973. All the buildings in this picture have been demolished including those in the background and the site is occupied by the Bridgewater Hall concert venue. Central station, with its enormous curved trainshed roof, closed in 1969 but survives, having been converted into the Manchester Central exhibition and conference hall. (W Ryan/Online Transport Archive)

A Manchester bus station which still exists is Piccadilly or Piccadilly Gardens as it is called nowadays which runs parallel to Parker Street. This facility originated in 1931 on the site of the former Manchester Infirmary and has been extended and modernised at various times ever since. It is now regarded as a transport interchange because it also serves the Metrolink tram system. The stands in this picture constituted an extension of the bus station over a truncated part of George Street. Occupying the foreground is former Manchester Corporation Transport 4400, a Daimler CVG6 with Metro-Cammell body built in 1953. Manchester was another of the eleven municipalities whose bus fleets were taken over by SELNEC on 1 November 1969. This bus retained its 4400 fleet number following the transfer and is still in Manchester Corporation livery as seen here in the 1970s. The buildings on the right which are situated in Mosley Street are still in situ and are now served by trams as well as buses. The classical style building with four Corinthian columns (10 Mosley Street) was built in 1836 and is Grade II Listed. The unusual building on the left (Bernard House/Eagle Star House) was built in 1973 and demolished in 2001. (W Ryan/Online Transport Archive)

Mansfield in Nottinghamshire was unusual in that, prior to amalgamations following integration into NBC in 1969, four major bus operators had garages in the town. These were Mansfield District, East Midland, Trent and Midland General. All but the last company are represented in this late 1970s view, Trent being the owner of the poppy red bus in the background. The bus station, located at Stockwell Gate North, was built in 1977 but the stands lacked outdoor waiting facilities. A new bus station was opened in 2013 on the Station Road car park with an elevated covered walkway to Mansfield railway station. The old bus station was converted into a temporary car park pending redevelopment and a hotel is now planned for the site. The bus seen in the foreground of this picture is Mansfield District 648, a 1965 Bristol Lodekka. (Alan Murray-Rust/Online Transport Archive)

This bus station in Castle Street, Merthyr Tydfil, South Wales, has been in place since the 1960s but is now deemed to be a poor gateway to the town. By Spring 2021 it should have been replaced by a new one in Swan Street sited closer to the railway station (just a four minute walk away). This picture portrays Merthyr Tydfil Corporation 146, a 1966 East Lancs-bodied Leyland PD3/4 which operated until 1976. The Council set up a separate company in 1986 called Merthyr Tydfil Transport but this collapsed in 1989 when it became unprofitable and fell into Administration, with no purchaser prepared to rescue it. (David Christie)

Teesside Municipal Transport (TMT) 83 rests at Middlesbrough Exchange bus station while bus crews socialise in the sunshine. TMT was formed on 1 April 1968, being an amalgamation of the fleets of the Tees-side Railless Traction Board, Stockton-on-Tees Corporation and Middlesbrough Corporation. No 83, a 1959 Weymann-bodied Leyland PD2/40, previously belonged to Stockton whereas the Northern Counties-bodied Daimler Fleetline in the background, No 113 dating from 1962, came from Middlesbrough Corporation. The Exchange bus station was used exclusively by Corporation buses and United Automobile Services had its own separate bus station. Both were replaced in 1982 by a new combined station built partly on the site of the United one. The building dominating the streetscape in this picture is the Royal Exchange built in 1868 which was demolished in 1985 to make way for a flyover serving the A66 road. However, the ornate terrace in the background on the right still survives, being the Grade II listed Zetland Buildings in Exchange Square. (C Carter/Online Transport Archive)

This facility at Morecambe Battery may not have been termed a bus station but its replacement in Central Drive, close to the railway station, is so described, yet merely consists of a few bus stops and shelters. The old bus terminus seen here in August 1974 was on the Morecambe/Heysham border in Heysham Road on a site mainly occupied today by a medical centre and pharmacy on the corner of Bold Street. Morecambe & Heysham Corporation buses did not use route numbers or display via points and visitors to Morecambe were probably puzzled by buses showing a destination of Battery. This was the name of a pub built in 1900 (now being converted into holiday apartments) sited behind the photographer and was named after a nearby former gun emplacement overlooking Morecambe Bay. This photograph was taken four months after the Lancaster and Morecambe & Heysham fleets were merged. The buses are carrying the new City of Lancaster fleetname but are still in their previous livery. The bus turning into the station is Massey-bodied AEC Regent V No 83 from 1956. No 84 is in the background behind the dog, standing alongside an older Regent III (No 69). The small window behind No 84 is the Inspector's office. (Mike Russell)

This little corner of Newcastle-under-Lyme bus station has vanished without trace even though there is still a bus station on this site, albeit considerably enlarged. The location is between Barracks Road (now a dual carriageway), Hassell Street and Stubbs Street but urban development and road alterations have entirely changed the surroundings. Newcastle-under-Lyme decided against joining the six local towns that amalgamated to form Stoke-on-Trent in 1910, preferring to remain independent. In this early 1970s view the bus nearest the camera is a PMT Albion Aberdonian with Willowbrook bodywork, built in 1957, one of 34 purchased by that operator. The bus on the extreme left belongs to Crosville which was using the bus station by this time. (W Ryan/Online Transport Archive)

With the opening of the Tyne Bridge in 1928 bus services were able to extend beyond Gateshead to Newcastle-upon-Tyne. In order to cope with the expected upsurge of traffic a bus station was required and consequently the one featured here was created in Worswick Street, relatively close to the bridge. The bus station was operated by the Northern General Transport Company (NGT) which built an adjoining office block, seen on the extreme right. Despite certain operational difficulties in later years (congestion, disabled access, passenger safety, buses protruding into the street, rear wheels needing to be chocked due to the slope, etc) Worswick Street remained in use for 68 years until it was closed in April 1996, replaced by one in Eldon Square which was more centrally located. The building then gradually fell into disrepair but was not demolished until January 2021. This view dates from November 1976, some ten years before NGT ceased operations following the privatisation of NBC which it joined in 1969. A variety of NGT buses feature in this view, the nearest being a Leyland Leopard which entered service in 1967 as No 2327. (Trevor Ermel)

Newport, Gwent, has two closely located bus stations in the Riverside area. This one is in Upper Dock Street (Market Square) outside the Victorian indoor market. The site, since reconfigured with buses facing in the opposite direction in herringbone pattern, is now used as Stagecoach's bus station and opened in 2013. The municipally-owned bus company, Newport Transport, operates from a nearby facility at the Friars Walk shopping and entertainment centre. The Company's buses are still green but this view shows some variations in the Council's previous green and cream colours originally introduced in the 1940s. The oldest livery visible is carried by the 1950 Guy Arab III, No 26, on the extreme left, behind 1957 Daimler CVG6 No 150. This latter bus was partially bodied by D J Davies but this company was unable to finish the work, which was completed in Newport's workshops. On the right is another Daimler CVG6, No 154 which is carrying a Longwell Green Coachworks body, a company which ceased to build bus bodies in 1960. The Leyland PD2/40, No 171, built in 1958 is also fitted with a Longwell Green body. (Roy Marshall/The Bus Archive)

Looking towards buildings in the left background which still exist in Newport's Corn Street, this is the site of the present Friars Walk bus station which opened in December 2015. The facility shown here was rebuilt in 1994 and demolished in 2014. This was the same year in which the adjacent Capitol multi-storey car park, out of view on the left, to which the footbridge is leading, was professionally blown up. When this picture was taken in June 1979, the bus station had long rows of bus stands but the facility was later reconfigured to the modern drive in, reverse out, herringbone arrangement. Newport Transport was a major operator of Scania buses, this one being No 60, a 1972 Metro-Scania BR111MH with MCW bodywork. (Alan Murray)

Norwich entered the modern road transport era in 1900 with a relatively short-lived electric tram system. Its demise occurred in 1935 following acquisition by the Eastern Counties Omnibus Company (ECOC) in 1933 although the tram offices in Silver Road, at the junction of Sprowston Road, built in 1907 as the Denmark Works of a shoe factory, still exist, converted into four town houses. ECOC purchased land between Surrey Street and Bull Lane in 1934 for a bus station and depot and the station opened to the public in 1936. A new, smaller bus station of striking design opened on the same site in 2005 and the Surrey Street backdrop of the early 1970s picture presented here is unchanged today although the bus station buildings on the right have been demolished. The ECOC bus in the foreground is LM617, an ECW-bodied Bristol MW delivered in 1965, withdrawn in 1978 and sold for further use. (John May/Online Transport Archive)

Huntingdon Street bus station in Nottingham was a large open air facility built in 1929, with bus shelters erected in 1949. Originally called the Central Bus Station when it was the only one, this appellation was dropped when Mount Street bus station was opened in 1944. A third bus station was created at Broad Marsh in 1952. Huntingdon Street closed in 1972 after a new facility and shopping mall was built on the site of the former Nottingham Victoria railway station which closed in 1967. This picture depicts W Gash & Sons' Massey bodied Daimler CVD6 which had its original 1948 Strachans body replaced in 1958. It has just pulled out of Platform 4 at the southern end of the bus station. The northern end on the left of this picture accommodated Platforms 5-8 and a bus park which can be seen at the rear of the CVD6 occupied by Barton and Trent vehicles. The indoor car park building originally housed the tramway's maintenance vehicles. (Phil Tatt/Online Transport Archive)

This is the northern end of Huntingdon Street bus station looking towards the front of the car park building. Platform 7 was used by Trent buses but No 1220, the 1951 Leyland PD2/3 depicted here, appears to be laying over rather than being available for service. At least it is parked to one side because there were often complaints from bus companies about other operators' buses laying over and blocking platforms, making it impossible for their own vehicles to reach the correct stand. Platform 8 on the left was used for express services and in this view is occupied by United Counties 470, an ECW-bodied Bristol LS6B built in 1953, which is waiting to take a service to London. A huge block of flats now stands on the bus station site. (Ron Copson/Online Transport Archive)

Oxford's Gloucester Green bus station opened in 1935 on part of the site of the Cattle Market after this had been resited. The bus station remains in situ, albeit in diminished size, having been rebuilt and reopened in 1989. The island cafe has been swept away and the bus station is surrounded by some new buildings of traditional appearance. However, the backdrop on the left behind the buses remains. The gabled structure is attached to "The Old School" and the chimneys belong to a terrace in Beaumont Street. This early 1970s picture highlights the distinctive livery of City of Oxford Motor Services' buses before the company was forced to adopt NBC corporate colours, in this case Poppy red. Standing at the front of Platform 1 is No 195, a Weymann-bodied lowbridge AEC Regent V of 1957 vintage followed by Bristol VRT No 901 from 1970, one of three originally ordered by Southern Vectis. On the right is a Bristol MW belonging to South Midland. (Geoff Morant)

It is August 1965 and two Devon General convertible open top buses have arrived at Paignton bus station, along with a Western National Bristol. The bus station exit is located opposite the railway station and the entrance seen here is beside the Grade II Listed former United Reformed church built in 1886 which stands on the corner of Dartmouth Road and Station Lane. The bus station has not moved over the years but was modernised in 2013. The two open top buses in this view, Devon General 926 *Sir Francis Drake* in front of 928 *Sir Humphrey Gilbert* (the latter vehicle having been preserved) belonged to a batch of nine MCW-bodied Leyland Atlanteans named "Sea Dogs". These were put into service in 1961 and operated until 1978 when they were replaced by a fleet of eight Warship class Bristol VRTs. The bus livery seen here is a reversal of the traditional Devon General maroon and cream colours. Devon General, which commenced bus operations in 1919, became part of NBC in 1969 and was merged with Western National in 1971 although the name continued to be used. (Mike Russell)

Bus stations could hardly be more inhospitable than this one in Station Square Perth, particularly in the pouring rain, although it did provide a rail/bus interchange, unlike the current one. With the railway station in the background and the Station Hotel (1 Leonard Street) on the far right (both of unchanged appearance today) this site is now an expanded surface car park and by the late 1960s buses had moved slightly further along Leonard Street to a proper bus station with covered shelter area and a cafe. However, this is now regarded as dilapidated and there is pressure for it to be replaced. When W Alexander & Sons was split into three regional companies in 1961, each adopted a different colour scheme for their buses and all three are on display here. The yellow (Northern) and red (Fife) buses are both Alexander-bodied Leyland Tigers from 1948 and on the right in blue and cream Bluebird coach livery is a 1958 Leyland Tiger Cub. On the extreme right is the side of a blue (Midland) bus. (Ian Dunnet/Online Transport Archive)

Bishop's Road bus station in Peterborough opened in 1937, a year after the Swimming Pool in the background (now Peterborough Lido) which is Grade II Listed. Bishop's Road itself is on the far left, identifiable by a passing lorry. This large open air bus station was replaced by a new one located in the Queensgate shopping centre in 1987. The original bus station site which contained a cafe located in its latter days within the shadow of the brutalist Magistrates' Court has been obliterated, partly by a new dual carriageway (Rivergate) and Peterborough Combined Court Centre, while the attractive Lido building lives on. In this view the front bus is a 1949 AEC Regent III which Longland of Crowland acquired in 1958. In a reversal of expected practice this Weymann-bodied vehicle started life as staff transport for Fison Pest Control of Cambridge prior to stage carriage service and ended up with Mulley's Motorways of Ixworth until going for scrap in 1975. Behind the Regent is a Bedford SB belonging to Green Coaches of Thorney. (Harry Luff/Online Transport Archive)

This is Bretonside bus and coach station in Plymouth photographed six months after it opened in March 1958, forming part of the massive rebuilding programme following the large scale destruction of the city centre in World War II. This scene is dominated by the brand new and subsequently Grade II Listed former National Provincial Bank building with clock tower in St Andrew's Cross. The bus station was also used as a general parking area for buses and coaches not necessarily picking up passengers here. In this view a variety of vehicles congregate. On the far left is Western National Leyland PD1A No 2929 and Plymouth City Transport 84, a 1957 Leyland PD2/40, while in the centre is a Western National Bristol LS6G coach from the batch with registration numbers LTA 874-8. Independent operator Heybrook Bay Motor Services, which was sold off at the end of 1958 due to the ill health of its proprietor, had a booking office in the station and the firm's Bedford SBO, RTA 97, is parked at its stand outside the office on the right. (C Carter/Online Transport Archive)

Bretonside bus station lasted almost fifty years before demolition in 2017 although plans had first been prepared nearly twenty years earlier for the reuse of the site. By the end of the 1990s the subterranean nature of the station, with passengers gathered under the Exeter Street viaduct, was regarded as being an unwelcoming gateway into the city and in 2016 a new coach station was opened nearby, with the remaining local bus services being relocated. Today, the view of Plymouth from this vantage point has changed dramatically. Huge buildings have been erected on top of the Exeter Street viaduct turning it almost into a tunnel. The remains of the ruined Charles church, completed in 1708 and virtually destroyed by incendiary bombs in 1941, dominates this scene. Constituting a memorial to the citizens who died in the World War II blitz the ruins now stand in the middle of a roundabout, somewhat overwhelmed by the surroundings. (Roy Marshall/The Bus Archive)

Tithebarn Street bus station in Preston is full of Ribble buses in this view from May 1950 apart from Scout Motor Services No 7, a 1949 lowbridge Leyland PD2/3. James Watkinson, founder of Scout, started charabanc tours in 1919 and had an uneasy relationship with Ribble until the outbreak of World War II when the two companies entered into a pooling arrangement and Scout were allowed into Tithebarn Bus station. Scout sold out to Ribble in 1961. Ribble opened this bus station in 1928 for its exclusive use but eventually other operators in addition to Scout were admitted. Following closure of the bus station in 1969 when the remarkable Brutalist building on the opposite side of the street was opened (see next picture) the site was cleared and part of it is now occupied by Preston Guild Hall. (C Carter/Online Transport Archive)

When this bus station in Tithebarn Street, Preston, opened in October 1969 it was the largest in Europe, with eighty bus stands, topped by a huge car park with iconic curved concrete balconies. Yet, from 2000 the building was threatened with demolition because it needed costly refurbishment, was too large and regarded as insufficiently central. It was reprieved in 2012, granted Grade II Listing in 2013 following two unsuccessful attempts, and refurbished in 2016-8, with the number of bus stands reduced to forty. This photograph was taken around 1971 and shows the Preston Corporation stands with buses carrying the later blue and white livery with the exception of the advancing Leyland PD2/10, No 26, built in 1956 which is still in the old maroon and cream colours. It is being followed by Corporation 215, a 1968 Leyland Panther. (W Ryan/Online Transport Archive)

Viewed from the car park and looking towards the Unicentre office block in Lords Walk, this was the side of Preston Central Bus Station used for Ribble, Fishwick and various coach services. The vehicle on the move is John Fishwick & Sons No 22, a Weymann-bodied Leyland Olympian built in 1957. John Fishwick started his first bus service in 1911 and the company went on to operate several routes from its base at Leyland until suddenly ceasing business on 24 October 2015. The refurbishment of the bus station has meant that the stands where the buses are parked on the extreme right of the picture, which were numbered 41-80, have been renumbered 1-40. Buses enter from Carlisle Street following the removal of the jagged-roofed buildings on the left. The area in front of the elevation facing Tithebarn Street depicted in the previous picture, formerly stands 1-40, has been turned into a public square. (W Ryan/Online Transport Archive)

The flowers are blooming around King Edward VII's statue opposite Reading General station in summer 1957. On the extreme right is Reading Southern station. Buses loaded on the station forecourt between the stations and also further along Station Hill to the left of the picture. Although this area was not officially designated a bus station it certainly acted as one. Later, the Thames Valley Traction Company had a covered bus station on Station Hill beneath the Top Rank Reading Suite which opened in October 1967 and was demolished in 2015 to make way for the recent Station Hill redevelopment. A new Reading railway station building has been built on the site of the Southern one and the former General station building has been turned into a pub. The double deck buses in this view all carry lowbridge bodies and consist of Aldershot & District Dennis Lance III No 127 (originally D732) built in 1949, and three Thames Valley Bristols. From left to right, these are No 594 (a 1950 KS6B) and KSW6Bs Nos 649 and 663. (Marcus Eavis/Online Transport Archive)

From a position in Chapel Street, Salford, Manchester, the photographer has captured the unattractive entrance to Victoria bus station which opened in December 1937. Its old green wooden bus shelters were replaced by modern steel ones in 1976. The bus station closed in 1988 but was briefly reopened in 2005 due to delays in completing the Shudehill interchange which opened for trams in 2003 and not for buses until 2006. The bus station site, which borders the River Irwell, is now a vast piazza. The five arches under the road (called Cathedral Approach) in the background are still visible and the gabled building in the background on the far right remains in situ. The buses are in Salford City Transport livery but are carrying their new SELNEC fleet numbers, 3114 and 71, the municipal fleet having been absorbed on 1 November 1969. The double decker is former Salford 268, a Leyland PD2/40 built in 1967 with a Metro-Cammell body and the single decker is ex-Salford 108, a Weymann-bodied AEC Reliance from 1962. (W Ryan/Online Transport Archive)

Former Salford City Transport 138, a 1962 Daimler CVG6 with Metro-Cammell lightweight Orion body, has acquired SELNEC livery and become their No 4027 in this scene from April 1973 as the bus departs Victoria bus station, Salford. Cathedral Approach above the arches led from Manchester Exchange railway station (in Salford!) to Manchester Cathedral (in Manchester!), the River Irwell creating the boundary. Manchester Exchange closed to passengers in 1969 and was later demolished, having boasted the longest railway platform in Europe at 2,238 ft (682 m). This was because one of its platforms was extended in 1929 to reach neighbouring Manchester Victoria station, thereby crossing the river from Salford to Manchester. In its day Victoria was a very busy bus station with ten stands. A large sign with the legend Salford Corporation Bus Station and later Salford City Transport Bus Station proudly reaffirmed that this was not Manchester! (Mike Russell)

Pond Street bus station in Sheffield opened in 1936 and received covered accommodation twenty years later. Until October 1959 trams operated along Pond Street and stopped alongside the bus station prior to closure of the tram system on 8 October 1960. The bus station was reconstructed in the early 1990s and received a name change from Central Bus Station to Sheffield Interchange. Some ten years later it was reduced in size due to insufficient usage. After this picture was taken in the early 1970s the main building was modified by the addition of a rounded section almost touching the "Threepenny bit" kiosk (incorrectly nicknamed as it was twelve sided whereas the coin was eight-sided!) Everything in this view has been swept away including the access bridge but the canopy supports on the far right remain. The bus nearest the camera is Park Royal-bodied Daimler Fleetline No 978 built in 1964 and, like the other buses depicted, belongs to Sheffield Corporation.

In addition to Sheffield Pond Street, there used to be several satellite bus stations aimed at reducing traffic in the city centre. One of these was Bridge Street bus station which was located close to the Tennant Brothers' Exchange Brewery (Whitbread's from 1961 until closure in 1993) which bordered the River Don. The bus station was situated opposite the junction of Snig Hill/West Bar and Bridge Street in an area which has been largely redeveloped and is now unrecognisable. In this picture from July 1983 the bus station is occupied by four South Yorkshire PTE vehicles. From left to right these are No 1715, a 1980 Alexander-bodied Leyland Atlantean, two Dennis Dominators with Alexander bodies (Nos 2127 and 2245 from 1981 and 1982 respectively) and an unidentified Marshall-bodied Leyland Atlantean. (Mike Greenwood)

Today's bus station in Shrewsbury is at Raven Meadows and is currently under threat. In the past it was located in Barker Street, split in two by Rowley's House which was built in the late 16th century. Midland Red used the upper part of the site while various independent operators occupied the lower section (see next page). This view dates from March 1969 and waiting passengers sit in the gloom about to be asphyxiated by a 1965 BMMO D9, No 5395, as it departs. This vehicle was withdrawn in November 1976. On the far left is another D9, No 5372, built in 1964. It was withdrawn in March 1976. Rowley's House stands behind the buses. The site is now a car park. (W Ryan/Online Transport Archive)

There is much of interest in this view of the lower part of Shrewsbury's Barker Street bus station as seen in June 1963. An elderly lady poses for the camera, a father collapses a push chair before boarding and a small girl hides between two buses. Adding to the scene are two unusual vehicles. On the left is a Harrington-bodied Commer Commando from 1949 operated by Albert Davies (Transport) Ltd of Acton Burnell, a company incorporated in 1943 and still active today in the road haulage business. On the right is a Crossley SD42 with Strachans bodywork built in 1949 and belonging to Mid-Wales Motorways, behind which is one of their double deckers. This area has also been turned into a surface car park and all the buildings in this picture are still standing. The terrace in the background is located in Hill's Lane. The building on the extreme right is Shrewsbury's first brick building, erected in 1618 for Roger Rowley's son and known as Rowley's Mansion. It stands next to Rowley's House. (W Ryan/Online Transport Archive)

Another depot which doubled as a bus station was the Eastern National (ENOC) one in London Road (A13), Southend-on-Sea. This one was built in 1968 with buses entering from Queensway (Southend Ring Road) at the back and exiting as seen here into London Road. It closed in June 1987 and was demolished to make way for a huge branch of Sainsbury's and associated car park. Following ENOC's integration into NBC on 1 January 1969 the lettering on the brickwork was changed to include the NBC logo. In this view a well-loaded Southend Corporation vehicle is leaving the bus station. It is Southend 217, a 1968 Leyland Leopard with an East Lancs body which was withdrawn in 1983. ENOC and Southend Corporation had a co-ordination scheme. (Howard J Piltz/Online Transport Archive)

This is a bus station inside an old railway station. Following closure in 1952 this part of Lord Street station in Southport was sold to Ribble which opened it as a bus station in June 1954, with the trackbed between the platforms having been filled in. The bus station was closed in October 1987 and the train shed roof was demolished in 1989. However, the station entrance building on Lord Street survives as part of a Travelodge. In this view the photographer is standing on the old platform 2 with the furthest steel barriers positioned close to where the buffer stops would have been located. In the background on the extreme left part of the street level entrance building is just visible. (Gavin Booth)

Out of all the scenes in this book, the one here at Stalybridge is probably the least altered. Apart from removal of the trolleybus wires, renewal of the shelters and a reduction in stands from seven to four, very little has changed, perhaps because this area was designated a Conservation Area in 1991, although that would hardly cover the bus station! Nevertheless, it is still in situ and remains open air and all the surrounding buildings are still standing. Ashbridge Motors is now a Bingo hall, the building behind the bus with the dormer windows is Thorn House in Waterloo Road which was built in 1904 and is Grade II Listed, and to its right is a former school, part of which is now a police station, dating from 1909. The picture was taken on the last day of Manchester trolleybuses, 30 December 1966, and the vehicle seen here is No 1334, a Burlingham-bodied BUT 9612T built in 1956 and destined to have a short life. The bus is a Northern Counties-bodied Daimler Fleetline belonging to SHMD. (Mike Russell)

In 1946 Stevenage in Hertfordshire was designated Britain's first New Town and in 1958 the Town Centre shops and new bus station by Danestrete opened. In 1980 when this picture was taken the area was largely unchanged but although the buildings and bus station are still in situ today change is on the way. Approval was given in June 2020 to the relocation of the bus station to Lytton Way, creating an interchange with the railway station. In this photograph local bus services were operated by London Country Bus Services, successor to London Transport's Country Department. The vehicles are carrying Stevenage Bus markings which was a rebranding initiated in 1980 to replace the previous Super Bus branding. This latter branding was introduced in 1971 for a range of flat fare, high frequency new local routes. The four buses featured here are all Leyland Atlanteans (AN class) and the one left of centre is Park Royal-bodied PDR 1A/1, AN70, which entered service in July 1972 and was withdrawn in August 1989, followed by scrapping. (Kevin Lane)

This general view of Mersey Square, Stockport, as seen from the Wellington Road South bridge (Grade II Listed and opened in 1826), is largely unchanged today apart from the removal of the bus station and the army tanks. All the buildings are still in place but the Mersey Tavern has become the Chestergate. The Art Deco building opened as the Plaza Super Cinema and Variety Theatre in 1932 and is Grade II* Listed. During the 1970s it became a Bingo club, as evidenced here, but has now been restored as a cinema. North Western used Mersey Square to terminate its fledgling bus services from the mid-1920s and a substantial shelter/office was constructed in 1927. Buses still frequent this area because of its proximity to the Merseyway Shopping Centre built on stilts over the River Mersey out of view on the left but since 1981 the bus station is now on the opposite side of the bridge in the area where North Western buses spent their layover and where the old Stockport Corporation depot was located. The bus in the centre of the picture is Ashton-under-Lyne Corporation 34, a Roe-bodied Leyland PD2/40 from 1963 with the unusual registration of 334 TF. Unlike other PD2s in the background this bus has yet to succumb to SELNEC livery and still carries its Ashton peacock blue and cream colours. The PD2 behind Ashton 34 is also still awaiting SELNEC livery as it remains in Stockport Corporation colours. (W Ryan/Online Transport Archive)

North Western Road Car Company buses occupy the starting blocks at Mersey Square bus station, with SELNEC vehicles bringing up the rear. However, autonomy for North Western was ending because on 1 January 1972 SELNEC took over North Western's vehicles and stage carriage services in its operating area which included Stockport. The three North Western buses pictured here are, from left to right, No 203, an Alexander-bodied Daimler Fleetline from 1966, No 909, a 1962 Leyland Leopard, also with an Alexander body, and No 970, a Park Royal-bodied AEC Renown built in 1963. The fleet numbers remained the same upon transfer to SELNEC. The buildings on the right and behind the AEC Renown have been replaced. The PLAZA name has been moved to the top of the building. (W Ryan/Online Transport Archive)

This is the bus station at Stockport which replaced Mersey Square, again photographed from the Wellington Road South bridge, but facing the opposite direction from Mersey Square. It opened on 2 March 1981 and won the Greater Manchester Transport's best kept bus station award in 1984. However, it is now out of favour and is about to be replaced by a new transport interchange to a modern design which avoids draughty bus shelters, as the ones seen here have been described. The buses in this view are branded Greater Manchester PTE which replaced SELNEC on 1 April 1974. The backdrop is one of the world's biggest brick structures, the Stockport Viaduct, completed in 1840 and Grade II* listed. It carries the West Coast Main Line over twenty-eight arches. The viaduct used an estimated eleven million bricks in its initial construction and a similar amount when it was widened. The huge structure was featured in the art of L S Lowry. (Roy Marshall/The Bus Archive)

This is Sudbury (Suffolk) bus station in Hamilton Road. Currently, it is virtually unchanged and although there have been recent plans to transfer it to Girling Street, this proposal has since been dropped due to overwhelming public opposition. The two buildings blocking the church tower remain in situ, as does the medieval Church of St Gregory. Passengers can be seen boarding Eastern National 1328 (originally No 502), an ECW-bodied Bristol MW5G of 1960 vintage. Standing alongside is ex-Halifax 16, an AEC Regent V subsequently acquired by Theobald's Coaches of Long Melford. Behind is a Duple-bodied AEC Reliance, 6801 HK, belonging to Rules Coaches of Boxford. This 1958 vehicle began its service life with Sutton's Coaches of Clacton-on-Sea. (Geoff Morant)

Today this bus would be parked in a pedestrianised part of Torquay alongside a landscaped area with palm trees. Torquay bus station has been removed as has the pub behind the bus which was the Marine Tavern, demolished in 1988. The road in the foreground is Vaughan Road and the long terrace is in Palk Street. The brick building on the extreme right is a bar and restaurant which straddles the corner of Palk Street and Vaughan Road. The bus is Devon General DL901, a Roe-bodied Leyland Atlantean dating from 1960. It is still carrying traditional Devon General colours despite its operator having been absorbed into NBC on 1 January 1969 but it would soon be repainted into the lighter NBC poppy red. (The Bus Archive)

Red and green London Transport RTs meet at Uxbridge bus station in August 1957. The bus station is located in Bakers Road at right angles to the Underground station with entry from Belmont Road seen in the background. The bus station is still in the same place but this scene is now unrecognisable. All the buildings visible have been replaced. In the foreground is Country Area RT 4547 which has an interesting history. The vehicle entered service in May 1955 so is just over two years old in this view and therefore in original condition. Therefore, it would not have received an Aldenham Works overhaul which almost certainly would have involved the body and chassis being changed and the fleet number being applied to a completely different vehicle. In 1950 the new Park Royal body which it is carrying was mounted on the specially adapted 1938 chassis of STL 2465 to become SRT 148 from 1950-1954. This was during a period when the delivery of RT bodies was exceeding the number of RT chassis being made. The red Central Area bus is roofbox RT 811. (Marcus Eavis/Online Transport Archive)

Above left: A new AEC Merlin with Strachans (pronounced Strawns) bodywork leaves Victoria Bus station on the first Red Arrow express route introduced on 18 April 1966 which pioneered the use of "standee" vehicles with limited fixed seating in London. Ironically, this bus seems to have had nearly as many identity changes as it had years of LT service: XMS 3, then MB 3 and finally MBS 3. Entering service in April 1966 and withdrawn in March 1973, the bus was bought by Dan Air and used at Gatwick Airport until being sold for scrap in July 1979. The bus station is situated outside Victoria railway station which was opened by the London, Brighton & South Coast Railway in 1860 but is seen here in its 1908 rebuilt manifestation. Kent services operated from a separate adjoining station. (Alan Murray-Rust/Online Transport Archive)

Left: The narrowness of the platforms at Victoria Bus station and consequent unsuitability for passengers with wheelchairs or pushchairs as well as creating a general safety risk, is clearly evident in this view dating from around 1970. The bus station, not to be confused with the Art Deco Victoria coach station of 1932, has undergone many alterations since the days of horse buses congregating here in the late 1800s. Developments which have come and gone include the installation of a watchtower by the London General Omnibus Company and a 1960s roof canopy removed in 2003. Approaching the camera is RM 2051, a 1964 standard Routemaster withdrawn in November 2004 and then sold. The building in the background is the Shakespeare, a hostelry first licensed around 1785 and rebuilt in its current form in 1870. (W Ryan/Online Transport Archive)

Above: With Wakefield's Cathedral spire looking as though it is attached to the bus station clock tower, this scene depicts the old site in Union Street which opened on 30 September 1952 and was funded by West Riding Automobile. Two of that Company's vehicles are on the left and right of this photograph: No 318, a 1971 ECW-bodied Bristol RE and Daimler Fleetline No 716 with a Northern Counties body from 1972. In the centre is Yorkshire Traction Leyland Leopard No 394 dating from 1964. This Marshall-bodied vehicle was new to County Motors (Lepton) as No 107 and joined the fleet of Yorkshire Traction in 1968 when this operator obtained control of County. A huge Market Hall now stands at this location leaving no trace of the previous buildings. A replacement Wakefield bus station opened on 25 September 2001, also situated in Union Street adjacent to the previous one shown here. (John May/Online Transport Archive)

These imposing buildings, which remain in place today, are part of the Seacombe ferry terminal in Wallasey from where services operate across the River Mersey to Liverpool. The terminal opened in this format on 10 April 1933 but, whereas in the past there would normally be several buses lined up in herringbone fashion creating the appearance of a bus station, there are now just a few bus stops and buses enter, loop round and depart. This photograph predates the formation of Merseyside PTE which merged the corporation bus fleets of Wallasey, Birkenhead and Liverpool on 1 December 1969. With its windscreen open, the vehicle in the foreground is Birkenhead Corporation 263, a Weymann-bodied Leyland PD2/12 of 1954 vintage. Behind is Wallasey Corporation 32, an Albion Nimbus NS3AN with Strachans bodywork built in 1962. Both buses were transferred to Merseyside PTE, retaining their existing fleet numbers. (David Christie)

This unusual photograph shows hoards of passengers at Seacombe ferry terminal/bus station and several buses all belonging to Merseyside PTE (MPTE). Tug boats fire hoses in the air as HM The Queen reviews the shipping on the River Mersey from the ferry, Royal Iris, the small vessel in the centre of the picture heading away from the camera. The date is 21 June 1977 and Her Majesty is paying a visit to Merseyside on the occasion of her Silver Jubilee. Sadly, the Royal Iris is currently lying derelict on the River Thames at Woolwich and appears to be beyond salvation. The three most visible buses in this view are, from the left to right, an ex-Birkenhead Northern Counties-bodied Atlantean and two Alexander-bodied Atlanteans new to MPTE. (R Barton/Online Transport Archive)

This birds-eye view of Walsall bus station in St Paul's Street dates from September 1978 and features nine West Midlands PTE buses, all of which are Daimler/Leyland Fleetlines except the one on the far right which is a Bristol VRT. St Paul's bus station was officially opened on 23 September 1937 with buses and trolleybuses occupying stands which were parallel to the backdrop rather than being angled, as seen here. A replacement St Paul's bus station opened on the same site on 2 August 2001 but is not universally liked. Photographs of the bus station taken around its opening in 1937 show the building behind the VRT bus and the newly built Corporation Transport Office on the extreme right in situ and both survive today. The other buildings behind the buses replace earlier ones but two famous retailers evident in the 1978 picture, British Home Stores and Woolworth, have vanished from our streets. Walsall Corporation Transport was subsumed into West Midlands PTE on 1 October 1969. (Steve Jones)

Until the opening of the first section of the Victoria tube line between Walthamstow and Highbury & Islington on 1 September 1968 there were no bus services terminating at Walthamstow and no need for a bus station. With the extra traffic generated by the new tube line a bus station was planned to open simultaneously but its completion was delayed and last minute temporary arrangements had to be made which involved the placing of dolly stops along a nearby residential street, Stainforth Road. The 1968 bus station, depicted here in summer 1975, involved buses making a U-turn (the tyre marks are visible in this view) because the road behind the photographer, Selborne Road, was blocked off. That situation remains even for the updated versions of this bus station which came into use in 1987 and 2004. Both the buses nearest the camera had short LT lives. AEC Merlin MB 638 entered service in August 1969 and was withdrawn in 1976. Daimler Fleetline DMS 1849 entered service in June 1975 (so is brand new here) and withdrawn in 1983. Both were sold on for further use before being scrapped. (Geoff Morant)

Above: Warrington bus station on Golborne Street, the location in this view, opened on 16 May 1979, forming part of the old Golden Square Shopping Centre, and closed on 20 July 2005 followed by immediate demolition. Temporary facilities were provided until the new Warrington Interchange opened on 21 August 2006. The bus station at Golborne Street had replaced a large open air facility at Arpley, whereupon all Crosville and Lancashire United services were transferred to Golborne Street. Warrington Borough Council is one of the few municipalities which wholly owns an arm's length company. Called Warrington Borough Council Ltd, the company currently trades under the name of Warrington's Own Buses. In this picture taken before local authorities were required to set up separate transport companies in 1986, the Council's Leyland Atlantean No 9 takes on a prospective passenger. This East Lancs-bodied vehicle was built in 1978 and is painted in the traditional deep red and ivory livery. In the background is a Crosville Bristol VRT. (Roy Marshall/The Bus Archive)

Above right: Welcome to Waterfoot bus station! This must be the most minimalist terminus in the book, if not in the whole of Great Britain, to be designated, according to the sign, a bus station by somebody, possibly the local council. Waterfoot is in Rossendale and the shelter is attached to the wall of 3 Burnley Road East, currently a butcher's shop. The picture was taken in February 1981 and this scene looks exactly the same today except that the "bus station" has been replaced by a normal roadside shelter and bus stop. The bus is Rossendale 53, an East Lancs-bodied Leyland Leopard dating from July 1968. The relevance of the date is that on 1 April 1968 the municipal fleets of Rawtenstall and Haslingden were merged to form Rossendale Joint Transport Committee. An arm's length company was set up in 1986 and this was sold by Rossendale Borough Council in 2017. (Jonathan Cadwallader)

Right: Pride of place at West Bromwich bus station on 22 March 1973 is taken by West Midlands PTE 174H, a 1952 Weymann-bodied Daimler CVG6. In this view, the bus is still in West Bromwich Corporation's elaborate colour scheme as it is today at the Black Country Museum following preservation. 1973 was its final year of service and it was frequently used for weekday evening peak journeys due to the unreliability of more modern vehicles. On this occasion it had been on driver training duty earlier in the day before undertaking a timetabled passenger service to Great Bridge and is seen here having its blinds changed. In the background is the PTE's Park Royal-bodied Daimler Fleetline No 4246 dating from 1973 and former West Bromwich Daimler CVG6 No 206 from 1957. The bus station was built in 1971 as part of a shopping centre development and was replaced by an updated version sited nearby in 2002, creating an interchange with West Midlands Metro trams. (Mike Russell)

Above: West Croydon bus station in Station Road has, like many others, undergone updating over the years. The version seen here in 1973 was replaced in 1983 and this was superseded in 2016 by an elegant new one which has received many plaudits. A tram stop has been placed opposite the current facility and in 2012 an entrance to West Croydon station was installed in Station Road (ironically alongside the former c.1860 station entrance building, now used by a car parts retailer) creating more of a transport interchange than existed previously. In this view from May 1973, a variety of London Transport and London Country vehicles are evident. From left to right the identifiable ones are RT 354, AN 28, RM 2197 and RM 1157. The bus station now has a slightly different aspect due to the encroachment of high rise office blocks. The building in the centre background is St Mary's Catholic Church in Wellesley Road. (Chris Evans)

Above right: In the 1930s an opening was created between 160 and 163 High Street, Winchester, facing the 1875 Guildhall and fronted by an archway. This heralded the Hants and Dorset Motor Services Ltd Omnibus Station. The archway remains with updated wording stating Winchester Bus Station and the facility reopened in September 2017 following renovation which included the demolition of the depot building seen in the background of this view from February 1974. Although it appears that people are walking through the depot from the road behind it is more likely that they have alighted from a bus parked behind the green one, otherwise they would be ignoring the No Admittance sign on the pillar below the clock. The bus, Hants & Dorset 1384 (1332 on entry into service in 1952) is an ECW-bodied Bristol KSW6B in its final year of service which is unsurprising, given the appalling state of its roof. The route number oddly appears in both front blind apertures. (Mike Russell)

Right: Overshadowed by the huge Victorian pub of 1900 in Railway Street, The Prince Albert, Wolverhampton bus station is seen here in the early1970s in one of its various manifestations. Rebuilt in 1986 and again in 2011 it is now located in nearby Pipers Row to form part of the new Interchange with the recently reconstructed Wolverhampton railway station (the former High Level one) and the upcoming West Midlands Metro tram line. From this angle, the pub is now hidden behind a huge multi-storey car park built on the bus station site. The original carriage entrance to the station (the Grade II listed Queen's Building built in 1849) which formed part of the previous bus station is now a coffee shop beside the new version. The building in the left background and still standing today is the Britannia Hotel. Turning now to the buses, West Midlands PTE had taken over these Wolverhampton Corporation buses as of 1 October 1969. The Guy Arab V has been repainted but the vehicle in the foreground, Strachans-bodied AEC Swift No 711 built in 1967, is still in Wolverhampton colours but with PTE fleetname. (W Ryan/Online Transport Archive)

Newport Street bus station in Worcester which closed in 1992 came to be criticised for its draughty concrete shelters but they look surprisingly smart in this early 1970s view. The school children do not appear to be particularly interested in Midland Red 5380, a 1964 BMMO D9 which remained in use until July 1976. It is operating a service to Birmingham on the famous 144 route which originated in 1914 following Midland Red's acquisition of the routes of the Worcestershire Motor Transport Company. However, the vehicle behind, a CM6 coach, would offer a faster journey to Birmingham according to its roof boards which carry the wording Birmingham Worcester Motorway Express. (W Ryan/Online Transport Archive)

BMMO C5 No 4829, a 1961 coach that has been downgraded and which lasted only ten years in service, leaves Worcester's Newport Street bus station on a Midland Red service to Bewdley. The bus station was demolished when the new covered facility beneath the Crowngate shopping centre multi-storey car park opened in 1992. This shopping centre replaced the 1960s Blackfriars shopping centre and resulted in the demolition of the multi-storey car park in the background of this view. A landmark feature of the old bus station was the roof mounted clock which is visible above the C5 bus in the centre of the picture. The site is now used as a car park. (W Ryan/Online Transport Archive)

Wrexham is in North Wales and borders Cheshire in England and this is the typically 1960s style bus station which was replaced on the same site in 2003. With Trinity Presbyterian Church of Wales in the background, Chaloner's one and only bus is running the operator's single route from Moss and Summerhill and is proceeding along King Street. The vehicle is a Willowbrook-bodied Bedford SB5 new to Chaloner in 1976 and withdrawn in 1992, followed by scrapping. Tim Chaloner obtained his first bus in 1929 and following his early death in 1946 the firm became D Chaloner and Son (widow Doris and son Edward). This unique bus service was taken over by GHA Coaches in 2003. (Roy Marshall/The Bus Archive)

Under the watchful gazes of a group of teenagers and a bus crew at Wrexham bus station, the photographer has captured on film two identical Bristol LWL5Gs belonging to Crosville Motor Services although they have different blind box operating handles. The picture was taken in 1970 and the buses are in their final year of service after nearly twenty years of operation. From this angle the massive replacement bus station building now blocks the view of the buildings in Trinity Street making up the backdrop, all of which are still standing. The new bus station which has received improvement works in 2013 and also very recently, has eight stands. Odd numbers are mainly under cover on the Trinity Street side while the even number stands are more exposed, with buses using a lay-by in King Street. (W Ryan/Online Transport Archive)

Yeovil bus station, viewed from the adjacent multi-storey car park, in August 1986, faces an uncertain future. The Glovers Walk shopping precinct, of which the bus station forms a part, was built in 1967 and is now generally regarded as outdated. As part of a town centre regeneration plan there are proposals to redevelop the site and it is uncertain whether the bus station will be retained or replaced. Since this photograph was taken the bus shelters have been redesigned to offer better protection to passengers and larger buses now operate from the facility. In this scene, two Southern National Ford Transit minibuses are plying their trade. Southern National's operations were transferred to Western National after they were both taken over by NBC in 1969 but the Southern National brand was revived in 1983 when Western National was split up in preparation for privatisation. The empty loading bays were generally used by various operators of country routes whereas the stands occupied by the minibuses were normally used for local services when this picture was taken. (Alan Murray)